THE BIG
PICTURE

THE BIG PICTURE

WHY DEMOCRACIES

NEED JOURNALISTIC

EXCELLENCE

JEFFREY SCHEUER

Routledge
Taylor & Francis Group
New York   London

Routledge
Taylor & Francis Group
270 Madison Avenue
New York, NY 10016

Routledge
Taylor & Francis Group
2 Park Square
Milton Park, Abingdon
Oxon OX14 4RN

© 2008 by Taylor & Francis Group, LLC
Routledge is an imprint of Taylor & Francis Group, an Informa business

Printed in the United States of America on acid-free paper
10 9 8 7 6 5 4 3 2

International Standard Book Number-13: 978-0-415-97618-3 (Softcover)

Library of Congress Cataloging-in-Publication Data

Scheuer, Jeffrey, 1953-
    The big picture : why democracies need journalistic excellence / Jeffrey Scheuer.
      p. cm.
    Includes bibliographical references and index.
    ISBN 978-0-415-97617-6 -- ISBN 978-0-415-97618-3 (pbk.)
    1. Journalism--Political aspects. 2. Press and politics. 3. Journalism--Objectivity.
I. Title.

PN4751.S32 2007
070.4--dc22
                                         2007017261

Visit the Taylor & Francis Web site at
http://www.taylorandfrancis.com

and the Routledge Web site at
http://www.routledge.com

For my parents

CONTENTS

ACKNOWLEDGMENTS

There are many fine books and articles about the media and democracy (separately and in conjunction) and I owe many intellectual debts. The selected bibliography lists some of these sources of challenge, correction, and inspiration for my work. A full bibliography is available on my Web site: www.jscheuer.com. Although works on journalistic excellence per se are few, a number of exceptional books about journalism's mission and public trust have appeared in recent years, including those by James Fallows, Samuel G. Freedman, Herbert J. Gans, and Bill Kovach and Tom Rosenstiel. Other sources of inspiration have included Robert A. Dahl, Norberto Bobbio, Robert M. Entman, Robert W. McChesney, Todd Gitlin, and Michael Walzer. The late Neil Postman and James W. Carey gave enormous lift to the entire enterprise of understanding the media.

Most of my teachers and critics have spoken to me via the printed page. Several others, such as Rob Richie of FairVote, and Andrew Schwartzman and his colleagues at the Media Access Project, have inspired me by example. And although I try to avoid media criticism in these pages, my friend John Rudolph supplied a timely example of journalistic excellence with his award-winning program, "Feet in Two Worlds," on radio station WNYC in New York. So did Michael Massing, an exemplary journalist and media critic. Among friends and mentors who have helped and guided me personally and generously, Mitchell Cohen and Victor Navasky deserve special thanks.

Dean Nicholas B. Lemann of the Columbia Graduate School of Journalism was kind enough to speak with me about his school, and also to share his 2003 Report to the Bollinger Task Force, and for both I owe him thanks. I would also like to thank James Boylan, who read a chapter of this book and provided many wise suggestions for improvement. I wish to thank my editor, Matthew Byrnie, and my extraordinary agent and friend, Mary Evans, for their help and patience, and Hilary Claggett and Jim Reische for their early enthusiasm.

Thanks also to Tanuja Gupta, Licia Hewett, and Alexandra Lincoln for providing valuable research assistance; to Simone Bien-Aimé and Adam MacLean, who always help and smile; to Lewis McDuffie, without whom it would all fall apart; and to my sister, Judith Scheuer, for a timely memento of shared memories of the Nevada pines.

I would like to thank Sal Fallica and Terry Moran, of the Department of Culture and Communication at New York University, for inviting me to deliver a lecture in 2002, which formed the basis for this book, and John Lang for the opportunity to teach a course in that department in 2003, as well as for his help in preparing to teach that course. For exceptional editorial assistance, I thank my mother, Marge Scheuer, and Richard Osterweil. I thank Heidi Rotterdam not only for valued editorial input but for the far greater gift of sharing her life and mine.

Finally, I would like to thank four institutions that have nourished my work over the years: the McCabe Library at Swarthmore College; The New York Public Library; the New York Society Library; and the Elmer Holmes Bobst Library at New York University. These magnificent sanctuaries summon Frost's hopeful words:

Here are your waters and your watering place. Drink and be whole again beyond confusion.

INTRODUCTION

One forgets so quickly one's own youth: once I was interested myself
in what for want of a better term they call news.

— Graham Greene, The Quiet American

I. The Media Labyrinth

This book is about journalism and democracy. More specifically, it is
about their complicated relationship, for they are deeply involved with one
another while also having separate lives of their own. It begins with this
modest bit of reasoning: If journalism serves a core democratic function,
without which democracy itself is all but inconceivable, then journalistic excellence must also factor into the quality of democracy. Journalistic
excellence — and not just freedom of speech and the press — must be
a basic democratic value. It cannot be a precondition of any democracy,
especially before we have defined what we mean by "excellence." But some
sort of journalism is necessary; and the quality of any democracy, to the
extent it can be measured or characterized, is at least partly determined by
the quality of its journalism. That is where our inquiry begins.

It is not a wholly mysterious notion. Knowledge is a form of power in
all societies, but most of all in democracies, where, at least in theory and
law, it is more widely diffused among the citizenry than elsewhere. Journalism is the most immediate and accessible source of such knowledge.
So the quality of information matters: how well it is gathered, selected,
organized, transmitted, and received. What people know, the accuracy
and extent of their understanding, bears directly on their ability to function as citizens.

Journalistic excellence is thus neither indifferent to democracy nor
merely an important adjunct. It is rather a component part, interdepen-

dent with other parts. That is the "Big Picture" — the complicated knot of issues, contentions, connections, and distinctions surrounding the role and functioning of the news media — that we shall explore. A central theme is that *democracy and journalistic excellence rise or fall together*. They are not just accidental neighbors; they are joined at the normative and conceptual hip. There can never be much of one without the other. That is not to say they fit comfortably or neatly or that everyone will like it. As we shall see, their joinder involves some interesting tensions — if not actual contradictions.

The journalistic enterprise is complicated enough without even considering the matter of quality and what makes it worthy of judging as good, bad, or indifferent. In attempting to reflect the passing social world, it also constitutes a vast counter-world of reproductions, like the shadows on the wall of Plato's cave. Or, to use a more current analogy, we might think of Einstein's parable of the moving train and the relativity of time as explained by Bertrand Russell in *The ABC of Relativity*: the news media attempt to take pictures from that train, and the pictures are useful — indeed, they are necessary, for lack of any better means of understanding where we are and the apparent motion around us. Yet, both subject and object are in motion; each "photograph" records just a tiny, imperfectly focused segment of the passing scene, and only of that scene; each artificially freezes the image in time so that it may be reexperienced by the audience (a kind of TV dinner of sound bites).

Each report is old when it reaches that audience; each is relative to the indefinable point of view of the "photographer" at the time of its execution; each is prey to the biases and preconceptions of both the photographer and the viewer of the picture, if not also to biases within the medium itself. And don't forget the moving train.

We know what the media do: they mediate; and different media mediate differently, but not always in obvious ways. But how do they fit into the social universe? Do they merely reflect or "photograph," or do they also distort, filter, spin, invent, suppress, disguise, oversimplify, overcomplicate, exaggerate, and obscure? Are they mirrors, or labyrinths? Are they mere adjuncts to society or lenses without which there is not a society to be seen? What is truth, and what is knowledge, and can they be separated from human values? Is the journalist a public servant, or what Hildy Johnson in *The Front Page* called "a cross between a bootlegger and a whore"?

What these complexities suggest is that an overview of journalistic excellence would require the combined skills of media critics, journalists, and scholars. It would have to explore a vast array of questions on many levels, of which these are just a few: 1) the professional and other qualities that distinguish the great journalist; 2) the specific strategies, ideas, values, and practices that produce the best journalism; 3) the organizational, cultural, and other hallmarks of great news organizations; 4) the proper standards of media criticism and its role in sustaining journalistic excellence; 5) the moral principles relevant to journalistic practice and criticism; 6) how journalists should be educated for excellence; 7) how journalistic excellence relates to politics and ideology, to issues such as bias, objectivity, advocacy, partisan debate, and to democratic ideals in general; and 8) the role of news within the broader culture of a democratic society, including its relationship to education, politics and law, economics, the arts, and other spheres of knowledge, entertainment, and imagination.

These are just some of the questions swirling around the moral and political role — the ultimate purpose — of journalism and journalistic excellence. We will touch on some of them in passing. If we think of this subject as a complex edifice with many levels, our focus will be most of all on the foundation, and how it fits into the landscape of democratic society.

2.   The 'Weak Slat'

Excellence is a word normally associated with moral and political neutrality. While the term *moral excellence* is sometimes used to signify an ideal of right conduct, it is hardly self-explanatory. It rather assumes some weighty notion of what precisely constitutes excellence in ethical conduct, that is, conduct vis-à-vis other human beings. It is linked to values such as altruism, honor, sacrifice, and conscience.

On the other hand, terms like *scholarly excellence,* or excellence in neurosurgery or most other activities, tend to connote something neutral and uncontroversial, insofar as they do not engage questions of moral or political value. We think of excellence in boat-building, aircraft design, or medicine as ideals of general value to society as a whole. How we achieve them, for whose benefit, and at what cost to whom, are separate and more politically charged questions.

Journalistic excellence is something else again. It involves more than just the attainment or approximation of an uncontroversial goal. It is complex, multifaceted, and somewhat vague. It is neither an art nor a science. And it is questionable whether government or the public at large can do much of anything to promote it. Yet for all that, it is intrinsic to democracy itself.

Unlike neurosurgery, journalism has very different implications when practiced in the United States, Egypt, or China. Those differences are not simply cultural; they pertain to the character and scope of democracy in those countries, and to the profound symbiosis between journalism and democratic values. That symbiosis, as we shall see, defines and complicates the notion of journalistic excellence. It is not just an ornamental feature of any model of self-government, but a basic supporting structure.

A. J. Liebling aptly identified journalism as the "weak slat under the bed of democracy." The questions I aim to explore are: why is it the weak slat, and what is it doing under this particular bed anyway? What exactly — or inexactly — *is* journalistic excellence? And if it is so important to democratic societies, how can they get more of it?

In America as in many societies, journalism reflects a contradiction between the imperatives of capitalism and the market, on one hand, and those of democracy and the public good on the other. By "contradiction" I do not mean that they cannot coexist without one devouring the other, but rather that, while they coexist, and on some levels even reinforce one another, they also contain oppositional, if not antithetical, tendencies.

More about this in due course; for now, suffice it to say that democracy is an engine of a certain kind of equality, whereas capitalism is an engine of a certain (different but not wholly unrelated) kind of *inequality*. Because there is both an economic demand for news and a political demand for it, journalism functions in both spheres at once, and is a nexus where those tendencies conflict.

Capitalism and democracy are both flexible social systems, capable of functioning at different levels and accommodating each other in different ways. The economic marketplace does not ensure any particular level of quality, quantity, or equality of access to information. (Equal knowledge would be too much to ask for.) At best, the market provides a general or chronic balance between information supply and demand. That, after all, is what markets do.

Most of the questions about media and politics that we shall explore flow from this intimate but conflictual relationship between those stubbornly indifferent markets and democratic ideals and institutions. What are the informational needs of a democratic society, and what are the public's legitimate claims on privately owned news media? Put another way, what are the public obligations of private media? And if those obligations are unmet, or those needs unsatisfied, how otherwise may they be satisfied?

The core dilemma may be described as follows. Democracies require informed citizens (the more informed, in general, the better); and the better the information, the better the quality of political discourse and decisions. But for both economic and political reasons, the state is not satisfactory as a primary source of information: most obviously, because we need independent information *about* the government, and news in general that is not propaganda. Otherwise, we could allow the government to collect our news just as it collects our taxes or our garbage. At the same time, however, private-sector, market-driven news production does not necessarily ensure optimal informational quantity, quality, or associated values, such as diversity, public access, or local news coverage.

To what extent can a democracy afford to franchise its information flow to the private sector? To what extent, in doing so, does it privatize and commercialize democracy itself? Is it analogous to private spending on political campaigns and the privatization and commercialization of elections? Does a rigid laissez-faire approach to information, however anchored in the First Amendment and wariness of state propaganda, indenture us to corporate-controlled news? What are the alternatives to those extremes?

3. The News-and-Democracy Paradox

High-quality journalism is not extinct or on the verge of extinction. However, it is fast becoming a ghetto within American culture, and a shrinking ghetto at that, with a smaller audience and blurred and contested boundaries. There will always be isolated patches of excellent reporting and analysis, and thoughtful opinions. Yet they are increasingly drowned out of the culture at large, marginalized by ambient noise, sound bites, and polemic.

Likewise, there will always be a market for excellence, if it must be marketed; to market anything is to alter, if not dilute, it to please the most buyers. But that market is shrinking, and more and more Americans are willfully choosing to remain ignorant. In the torrent of emotion-centered, hyper-commercial media, democracy and journalistic excellence have experienced a joint downward spiral: not toward death but toward their marginalization. They have simply become sideshows.

Nowhere in the U.S. Constitution does it state that there must be news. Except for the blanket proscription of government abridgement of freedom of the press in the First Amendment (and granted, it is a big exception), there is nothing that establishes the press as a "fourth estate," in effect a branch of government. Yet the news media serve at least three critical, widely recognized, and overlapping democratic functions: first, informing the people generally; second, holding government and other sectors accountable to the public, by serving as a "watchdog"; and third, sponsoring public discourse and debate.

The First Amendment does enshrine the general rights to freedom of religion, speech, the press, and assembly — although, notwithstanding its absolutist language, the First Amendment has been subjected to two centuries of legal interpretation, limiting those rights in various ways and affirming them in others. The Constitution is silent, however, about how exactly Americans might meet any information needs arising from self-government — or whether they even have such needs. It does not mandate that the press should exist at all, much less that it do a good job; it only stipulates that, if any such press exists, it should be (more or less) free of governmental intrusion. Simply put: we could, consistent with our Constitution, have no journalism at all.

At the same time, the news media are not a historical accident, or an expression of human faith, or a gift of nature like sunshine and rain. Nor are journalists visitors from another galaxy (talk about objectivity!). So if we ask why the media exist, the most obvious answer would have to be brute economics, mixed with a dash of convention and cultural inertia: there is a popular commercial demand for news media and entertainment, and so there are media companies — from the *Wall Street Journal* to porn magazines — that supply it for profit.

Of course it is not quite as simple as that; public demand can be induced, cultivated, massaged, and manipulated up to a point. There are vast gaps and anomalies in the chain of accountability that the market represents. (That is why some TV journalists, like some ballplayers, earn far more than "what the market will bear" for their services — especially news anchors and relief pitchers.) But the existence of commercial news media reflects the fact that there is a market of some kind, however inefficient; some people do want to watch, listen to, and read news, and are willing to pay for it.

Citizenship, idle curiosity, peer status, self-image, boredom, the relentless desire to be stimulated or entertained — there is a range of motivations and appetites for news. Some people fear it or simply ignore it. Also, there are various kinds and grades of news, produced for more or less specialized audiences, variously intended to inform, manipulate, or beguile. So real news, almost by definition, cannot be intended purely for profit. There are easier ways of making money.

Why, in fact, do we need news at all? What would happen if there were no news, or if nobody bothered to consume it? Why does it matter how well it is gathered and produced, or whether it is produced at all? And what if no one paid attention? People obviously need certain kinds of information for their work or for narrower reasons: stock market quotes and business stories, sports, weather, society gossip, celebrity misbehavior, etc. But why do ordinary people need ordinary news? Among other reasons, people need news in order to be citizens, and to be consumers and economic and political agents in general. In a world based on money, law, and information, we need information first of all.

The impulse to disseminate information, to teach or transmit knowledge, is a basically egalitarian one (except when there is a profit to be made). It is less selling than sharing. Kenneth Minogue has written, "Like democracy, journalism is a manic equalizer."[1] This would seem to make journalism an essentially democratic function — or at least, a democratic as well as a capitalist one; it might even be dispositionally a liberal more than a conservative institution.[2] (I will not attempt to defend this assertion here, but offer it up as an initial sacrifice to the gods of disputation.)

Let us qualify it with a distinction: the urge to actively disseminate information is not what we're really talking about here, but rather the more general and passive interest in receiving it: the interest, that is, that information generally, or information of some particular kind, be disseminated. The impulse to disseminate may stem from an urge to deceive, to manipulate, to titillate, to swagger in the limelight, to exploit for profit, even to oppress. Or, it may be a desire to inform and educate. Journalism, of course, has always been an uneasy blend of these impulses — the disinterested urge to inform, and the naked urge to sell. Which brings us to back to our main question:

What is excellence, what does it mean in the journalistic context, and, finally, can it be bought and sold, in the bazaar of modern capitalism, and still satisfy the needs of democracy?

Many conscientious journalists will say yes, it can — whether out of honest conviction, through a veil of habit or self-defense, a belief in the "church-state" separation of business and editorial functions, or simply to validate their own work. They will defend the commercial model, arguing that news is indeed, and ought to be, a commodity; that it has a value that translates without distortion or loss into market value; that if it is not supported through the marketplace, where then will it derive its support? They have a point; certainly some of the best journalism in America is produced by commercial enterprises. We will not seek to demolish the commercial argument, but to show that it is too narrow: to blunt the journalists' point so far that it will start looking more like the eraser end of their pencil.

4.   Mr. Luce's Folly

Three salient moments in the history of the American media bear upon this investigation of journalistic excellence and democracy. The first is the debate between Walter Lippmann and John Dewey over the nature of democracy and the role of the press, pitting Lippmann's more elitist conception (*Public Opinion* [1922], *The Phantom Public* [1925], and elsewhere) against Dewey's more egalitarian and populist one (*The Public and Its Problems* [1927]). That debate opened up a range of important questions about the relations between democratic mass publics and elites, and the consequent role of the press.

It would take us too far afield to examine that debate in detail. But the conception of democracy advanced here generally follows in the Deweyan tradition, which holds that communication is not just instrumental to knowledge and democracy, but integral to them.[3] Democracy, for Dewey, is not just a form of government, but a broader and more complex web of communication — a storing and sharing of knowledge that forms publics or communities out of mere masses of individuals. Lippmann, in contrast, argued (with increasingly conservative conviction over the years) that the issues facing modern democracies are too complex for average citizens to fathom, suggesting that the main role of journalism is to service governing elites.

The second historical moment, and the least widely remembered, was the publication in 1947 of the Hutchins Commission's report, *A Free and Responsible Press*, the most significant independent study of American journalism ever conducted (which is not saying much).

The third moment, in a sense ongoing, is the public journalism movement, which during the 1990s raised the consciousness of the journalistic community about the civic duties of news providers. Although an important and largely salutary trend in American journalism, public journalism will not figure in our discussion, chiefly because the focus here is less on the content of the news, and more on the form and context; in addition, there is already extensive literature on that movement.

Each of these moments has left important residue. But the most useful touchstone for our themes is the Hutchins Commission's summary report on the responsibilities of the press. The seed of that report was planted in 1942 by the publisher Henry Luce, founder of Time, Inc. (He didn't care much for the taste of the final fruit, but that is another story.) At a wartime board meeting of the Encyclopedia Britannica, Luce passed a note to a fellow board member and former Yale classmate, Robert Maynard Hutchins, the eminent lawyer and educator and then-president of the University of Chicago, wondering what the responsibilities of journalists were to society. The note led to the formation of the Commission on Freedom of the Press, commonly known as the Hutchins Commission. Luce provided the bulk of the funding ($200,000), and the Encyclopedia Britannica, affiliated with the University of Chicago, later provided an additional $15,000.

The Hutchins Commission was one of the most august bodies of older white males ever formed on American soil. Its roster of thirteen commissioners, mostly scholars and lawyers, had close ties to Harvard, Yale, the University of Chicago, and to the New Deal. The group included, in addition to Hutchins, the theologian Reinhold Niebuhr; Archibald MacLeish, the diplomat, writer, poet, and playwright (and winner of three Pulitzer Prizes), serving at the time as Librarian of Congress; Harold D. Lasswell of Yale Law School; the Harvard historian Arthur M. Schlesinger; Zechariah Chafee, Jr., of Harvard Law School, a leading First Amendment scholar; John Dickinson, a professor of law at the University of Pennsylvania and general counsel for the Pennsylvania Railroad; Beardsley Ruml, chairman of the Federal Reserve Bank of New York; and William Hocking, professor emeritus of philosophy at Harvard.[4]

The Commission held some seventeen two- to three-day meetings between 1943 and 1946, conducting interviews and discussing among themselves the knotty issues of press freedom and responsibility. The commissioners argued not only about substantive issues but about the eventual publication's style, tone, and likely reception by the press. The chief result was a relatively brief (139-page) summary report, titled *A Free and Responsible Press*, issued (after some nine major revisions) in March 1947. Four other volumes, examining particular aspects of the media (radio, film, international media, and the First Amendment), were published separately.

The title itself, *A Free and Responsible Press*, aptly reflected the fundamental dilemma of democratic journalism. In any democracy the press must be free. Freedom is never absolute, as excesses by some can abridge the freedom of others; a free press may conflict with rights of privacy and reputation, for example, or with public safety or national security.

The cornerstone of American democracy, the First Amendment, declares that "Congress shall make no law respecting an establishment of religion … or abridging the freedom of speech, or of the press …" It is a negative proscription, stating only what must not happen. At the same time, if we cannot have a democratic society without news, it would seem that journalism has some particular responsibilities to society, entailing a positive need for something to happen. How can that circle be squared, so that the press meets its responsibilities without its own freedom being curtailed?

Despite the eminence of the Hutchins Commission, the report it produced was in many respects a failure, if not a comedy of errors. For one thing, although studded with academic and legal stars, the Commission contained not a single journalist — a glaring and apparently intended omission, which the press, in its response, did not fail to notice. (Hutchins reportedly defended the decision by claiming that including journalists would have made the panel "unwieldy.")[5] The panel conducted no systematic research, but simply interviewed journalists and others and discussed the results among themselves; and the slim summary report was no literary gem.

It is impossible to know exactly to what extent the report's credibility was undercut by the exclusion of journalists, or by its platitudinous style and windy arrogance. At times it achieved eloquence; at others it bordered on incoherence.[6] Furthermore, it failed to provide a clear statement of its purported goal, identifying the press's responsibilities, focusing more on the actual deficiencies of American journalism. Some of those attacks were gratuitous and unfair; the report was full of dark warnings (bound to raise the hackles of journalists) that if the press did not regulate itself to serve the American public more responsibly, the government would do so (which would be a violation of the First Amendment).[7]

Finally, for all its emphasis on the importance of liberal education (Robert M. Hutchins being among the foremost educators of his time), the Commission scarcely considered the state and purpose of journalism education. It alluded to journalism schools in one passage, with great disparagement, offering no ideas for reforming that institution to further journalism as a democratic service.

In much of the tabloid press, the report was vilified. Robert McCormick's *Chicago Tribune,* for example, ran its story under the headline: "A Free Press (Hitler-Style) Sought For U.S.: Totalitarians Tell How It Can Be Done."[8] This despite the fact that Hutchins had written in the Introduction:

> If modern society requires great agencies of mass communication, if these concentrations become so powerful that they are a threat to democracy, if democracy cannot solve the problem simply by breaking them up — then those agencies must control themselves or be controlled by government. If they are controlled by government, we lose our chief safeguard against totalitarianism and at the same time take a long step toward it.[9]

The questions raised by the Hutchins Commission about the responsibility of the press, the dangers of concentration and commercial influence, and paths to reform, were not altogether new. They were prefigured not only in the debate in the 1920s between John Dewey and Walter Lippmann, but also in the work of late-nineteenth and early-twentieth-century German social theorists such as Albert Schäffle, Karl Bücher, Ferdinand Tünnies, and Max Weber. The Commission's report lacks this historical perspective, and it also lacks perspective on its own time: the onset of the Cold War, which refocused American society on confronting the external threat of Communism, and on perceived internal threats. It was not the ideal time for bold reforms.

The reaction was not entirely negative, however. A. J. Liebling, reviewing *A Free and Responsible Press* in *The Nation,* wrote that he was at first "inclined to wonder uncharitably as I read the book what they had spent the $200,000 on." But he added that the work had "importance in the long struggle for a truly free press that is beginning all over again because of technical advances which have wiped out the old freedom of any effective journalist who could have a handpress to start an effective newspaper." Liebling concluded, "A chief service of the volume is that it makes criticism of the press respectable."[10] Walter Lippmann weighed in with support for the idea of an annual report on press performance, asking: "Who watches the watchman, who inspects the inspector, who polices the policeman?"[11]

Sixty years later, few Americans, even in the journalistic community, have even heard of the Hutchins Commission or its report. One of its ideas — for a national organization to hear complaints against the media and adjudicate claims of unfairness or inaccuracy — achieved brief fruition. The National News Council, formed in 1973, was boycotted by the *New York Times* and other elite news organizations; unable to secure further funding, it folded in 1984.

In short, the Hutchins Commission report was not the sort of document that would win much critical approval today. Considering the stellar quality of the individual commissioners, the report could fairly be judged a work of astonishing mediocrity.

Except for two things.

First, as Liebling presciently noted, the Hutchins Commission did set a precedent, helping to legitimize the practice of press criticism as an important activity for a mature democracy. It is impossible to gauge the report's indirect or delayed effects; but the *Columbia Journalism Review,* the nation's preeminent institution of media criticism, was founded fourteen years later, in 1961, at the Columbia Graduate School of Journalism, and others followed.

Second, and more to the point here: despite its obvious shortcomings and the vagueness of some of its conclusions, the Commission got just about everything else right in the end. It raised profoundly important questions; and it correctly discerned and concisely stated the democratic news imperative:[12]

> Today our society needs, first, a truthful, comprehensive, and intelligent account of the day's events in a context which gives them meaning; second, a forum for the exchange of comment and criticism; third, a means of projecting the opinions and attitudes of the groups in the society to one another; fourth, a method of presenting and clarifying the goals and values of the society; and, fifth, a way of reaching every member of the society by the currents of information, thought, and feeling which the press supplies.

The Hutchins Commission understood the crucial importance of news to a democracy — not just to its existence or survival, but to the quality of its functioning — and what a strong commitment to democracy requires of news media. With perhaps just a touch of overstatement, one writer later described the report as "a paradigm shift in journalistic emphasis: from press freedom to press responsibility."[13]

The Commission members no doubt sensed, but may have feared to express, just how difficult it is to render such critical relationships in terms of specific policies or principles, especially in the context of one of the world's freest press systems. But the report's conclusions, although some of them were too vague to be of much practical use, were the right ones for its time. And as I will suggest, they are the right ones for ours.

5.   Disclaimers, Evasions, and Cultural Criticism

In exploring journalistic excellence with special focus on its democratic context, this book aims to show, if nothing else, just how close to the mark the Hutchins Commission came in identifying the problematic information needs of a democratic public. We will approach the subject on several levels: looking first at the democratic foundations (Chapters 1 and 2), then at the intellectual foundations, considering core ideas of excellence, truth, knowledge, and ideology (Chapters 3 to 6); and finally considering the institutional bases of education and independence (Chapters 7 and 8).

Among other things, I hope to reinforce the notion that journalism, politics, and economics deeply interpenetrate and influence one another, and that journalism cannot be practiced with indifference to, or free of influence by, economic or political conditions. We may aim for journalistic neutrality — and there is a dignified and important role for it, as there is for advocacy. But we cannot pretend that it is a simple goal or even, in the end, an attainable one within the complicated social matrix in which journalism is embedded. Balance and fairness are important, and objectivity has its place. But the illusion of easy neutrality or broad objectivity is a blind alley, oversimplifying journalism's function as the principle source of timely civic education.

The emergence of the Internet, and with it the blogosphere, as a boundless new medium for interpersonal communication, appears to threaten the very existence of traditional journalism. It is one reason (among others) why the question arises: what if there were ordinary journalism but nobody came; what if the audience for newspapers, news magazines, and network television disappeared?

The blogosphere is nothing if not democratic (except for have-nots); anyone with a computer can yell into their electronic megaphone, or post a fascinating tidbit of autobiography on YouTube, regardless of who is watching or listening. But bloggers, thus far, do not report much from Iraq, or from Congress, the White House or City Hall, or from Wall Street or Silicon Valley; or from troubled inner-city schools or family farms, or from a distant, tsunami-ravaged coast. And if they do report on these, it is without quality controls. In the crudest terms, bloggers seldom make a living at it, or submit their work to editorial review, and they cannot be fired or sent away for more training. None of which is a ringing endorsement of the quality of traditional journalism; but would we want to replace schools, for example, with Wiki-style homeschooling?

Nothing guarantees the persistence of journalism with qualifiers such as "traditional," "professional," or "mainstream." And we do not need such ordinary journalism in order to feel part of a democratic community. We only need something like it to be effective democratic citizens. (But you may find intimations here of a different kind of "ordinary journalism" than what we are used to.)

Given the analytic range of this project, many important issues must be short-changed or left aside. The media's gate-keeping roles in setting the social, political, and cultural agenda; the specifics of the watchdog function as a means of keeping government and other sectors publicly accountable; the important public journalism movement, designed to focus journalism more on issues of civic relevance; the ambiguous portents of the Internet for journalism and for democracy — all of these deserve, and have received, considerable attention.

Similarly, we will not address the issue of media conglomeration and homogenization, which has been ably and thoroughly explored elsewhere, in particular by Ben Bagdikian and Robert W. McChesney. For that matter, the analysis of what the media cover and how — of news content, the selection process, journalism's accountability to its audience — are left to the more capable hands of media critics.

The critic identifies good and bad journalism and explains the difference; the philosopher explores the connections between journalism (or any other human enterprise) and theories of knowledge and reality. Both have their work cut out for them. Echoing the Hutchins Commission, I pose an intermediate question: what kind of journalism does a democracy need — in terms that ordinary citizens and journalists can use — and how can we get it?

The argument is in the form of an extended essay. Do not look in these pages for either logical deductions or abundant and specific factual evidence; the aim is to consider how journalism can best serve democracy and vice versa — and to understand why they share a common fate. It is an attempt to sketch the big picture, based on a series of considered assumptions and inferences. One such assumption is this:

The quality of a democratic society is jointly determined by its legal and constitutional framework, by the energy and public spirit of its citizens, and by the quality of its education and public discourse, and especially the education and discourse of journalism.

As suggested earlier, there are at least three general levels at which one might examine the issues of excellence in journalism: that of the individual journalist and his or her audience; that of the organization or institution; and that of society as a whole, with the broadest political implications. The focus here is mainly on the last. No doubt there are other important perspectives, and other ways of approximating what we might call excellence in a journalist, a news organization, or a society. The mind draws black on white, but the world is mostly gray. No democracy or media system is perfect, but some are better than others.

As such, I am taking what might, with due qualifications, be called a "cultural" approach to journalistic excellence. The qualifications stem from the vagueness of that term and its occasional abuse as an intellectual smokescreen for all sorts of pedantic nonsense. I do not mean to obfuscate. "Cultural" here means the exploration of the shared context of journalism and democracy, their conjunction in a domain broader than either one occupies in isolation. It means looking at democracy and journalistic excellence as parts of an ecological system, and not just through the narrower (but important) lenses of daily journalism, news consumption, or political science. It is a domain referred to by some as "media ecology," although the focus here will be on news production and not on other types of informative or entertainment media.

At least two conscious biases come with this approach. The first is intellectual. All political systems, but democracies most of all, are moving targets, and so are subject to the laws of relativity. Almost anything that can be ascribed to democratic systems (for example), or to the media, and how to improve them, is relative and incremental, a matter of degree and not either/or. Thus, for example, it is not the case that democracies are egalitarian and monarchies are not; rather, democracies are more egalitarian, and some more than others, but none perfectly so. Nor is all quality journalism or commentary found in traditional places. Nothing is absolute, although some things are categorical — but that is a different story. The mind is sometimes tidy, and can tidy up the world for the sake of understanding; but the world is always messy.

The second bias is moral and political. We understand "democracy" as a set of norms imperfectly embodied in various related systems of government: systems that are capable of evolving — not steadily or logically, but in lurching increments. In moving forward, democracies display a capacity to repair and expand themselves. An inner dynamic keeps them capable of moving closer to their own ideals. The promise (which is unattainable but also inextinguishable) is that democratic systems can unlock the synergistic energies of free people — cultural, economic, educational, religious, moral — to move to higher planes of life, based on political structures of equity, equality, openness, and inclusion.

Nothing that is said or written or done about media in a democratic society can ever be considered a finished work. Democracies and their media are always in flux, each influencing the other in a relationship that is necessary, complicated, and fraught. This book explores some aspects of that relationship. It is not just about what excellence means for journalists, audiences, or prize juries, but also the broader political and analytic context. Looking at the big picture, some important details will inevitably be lost or blurred; but, knowing that we stand on shifting ground, the view to that horizon may offer some recompense.

Endnotes

1. Minogue, "Jouralism: Power Without Responsibility," The New Criterion (Feb. 2005): p. 5.
2. 'Liberal' and 'democratic' are distinct as well as overlapping ideas, and typically conservatives are equally committed to the core concept of democracy, although not as committed to expanding democracy.
3. Because the focus here is on journalism, and on democracy as an anchor of journalism, it might be overstating to suggest that I am advancing a particular "view" of democracy, except insofar as I conceive it to involve the interaction between what I call the "hardware" of a legal framework and the "software" of an informal culture or civil society, notably including journalism.
4. Other Commissioners included Charles Merriam of the University of Chicago, one of the nation's leading political scientists; Robert D. Leigh, a former president of Bennington College, who headed the Commission's staff; and Robert Redfield, an anthropologist and dean at the University of Chicago.
5. M.A. Dzuback, Robert M. Hutchins: *Portrait of an Educator*, p. 222.
6. The Appendix, in particular, is a monument to philosophical obscurity. But the body of the report also contains lines such as the following on p. 118: "While dutiful utterance bears the burden of the claim of right as against the state, that right extends its coverage over all legitimate expression."
7. (Hutchins Report): On p. 79, for example, the Commission states that "The more the press and the public are willing to do, the less will be left for the state..."
8. Quoted in H. Ashmore, *Unseasonable Truths: The Life of Robert Maynard Hutchins*, p. 296.
9. Hutchins, "Freedom and the Responsibility of the Press: 1955," address to American Society of Newspaper Editors; quoted in Ashmore, op. cit., p. 297.
10. Liebling, *The Nation* (April 12, 1947), p. 427.
11. Lippmann: "Free for All: Freedom of the Press," Fortune, June 1947; quoted in *H. Ashmore, Unseasonable Truths: Robert Maynard Hutchins*, p. 296.
12. *A Free and Responsible Press*, p. 20.
13. ("Paradigm shift"): J.C. Merrill, *Journalism Ethics*; p. 14.

I

The Bed of Democracy

Democracy is always in trouble. Democracy has to be
defended every minute, every hour, every day, every year
... every generation has to solve its own problems.
                                                    — **Ben Bagdikian**[1]

1.   Foundations of Journalism and Democracy

Communication invites complexity, and like most forms of
communication, journalism has blurry boundaries and internal distinctions. Broadly speaking, it is the diffusion of topical
information from the (more organized and informed) few to
the (more disparate and less-informed) many. But it is not a
single thing — although it is a convenience, an economy of
meaning, to call a range of related things "journalism"; and
what we call "journalism" may also resemble things that it is
not, and may derive from various motivations.

One such motivation is instrumental and political, to serve
or please the powers that be, as with state propaganda (when
invented rather than reported, we tend not to call it journalism). Another is profit, as is the case for commercial news, paid
advertising, public relations, and infotainment. Political and
economic interests can corrupt information in many ways and
degrees; it often advances those interests to do so.

The purpose of serving democracy by informing citizens
seems implausible, because it disdains both power and money

as its aim. Who would want to do that? But perhaps the more pressing question is: how can there be any democratic society *without* such — to coin a phrase — "clean news"? To be sure, all journalism worthy of the name does not derive its rationale purely from the furtherance of democracy, that is, from the disinterested diffusion of topical information; and neither does all great journalism. Fortunately, at least some journalism, including some of the most important forms, serves democracy, however imperfectly. If it didn't, nothing else would.

For that matter, democratic constitutions do not call for institutions of higher education either. Governments may find it expedient to legislate public support for higher education, as the United States has done, beginning with the 1862 Morrill Land Grant Act, which founded land-grant colleges. But no one can doubt that whatever their flaws, public schools, financed by local government through property taxes, and the mostly nonprofit, privately founded (and often religious) institutions of higher education, are essential to American democracy as well as to American economic prosperity. The same may be said for public transportation and interstate highways.[2] Here the effects may be harder to measure. We can only imagine what a corrupt backwater America might be without its independent centers of learning and research.

Put another way: journalism does not "need" democracy as its sole rationale in order to exist; certain forms of journalism (usually limited and inferior) occur in nondemocratic societies. But, as we shall see in this chapter and the next, democracy does need journalism — at least of certain kinds, certain amounts, and perhaps even of a certain caliber. And so we begin the exploration of journalistic excellence by looking at its close, complicated, at times dysfunctional relationship to the family of democratic values.

In order to understand this relationship, it is not necessary to explore every nook and cranny of democratic theory, interesting though it is. Rather, we need to consider the critical importance within the framework of democratic ideas not just of freedom of speech but also of the diffusion of topical information generally (good, bad, and indifferent, but especially good) in sustaining a system of popular self-government.

We do not simply "create" informed public citizens. Neither do they spring into being fully formed (or fully *in*formed). Democracy is not just a plan or a set of principles, although it is partly that. It is also endless work; like a marriage, it is far more than a written contract. As marital "work" must be conducted in the private sphere, the work of popular government must be conducted in the public — and a significant part of it must be conducted out of the reach of either government or private interests. Maintaining the free flow of information is a critical part of that democratic work.

2.   Democracy and Its Concomitants

As with journalism, when we think of democracy in its modern forms we think of several related things. One is representative government, in which citizens are empowered through freedom of expression, assembly, and representative government. At the same time, democracy is a legal system designed to allow disagreement — and a system of belief in argument and voting as a way of accomplishing change, as an alternative to violence or fiat. It is about the separation of powers within government to ensure (or at least to further) the freedom and self-government of the people. So from one perspective, democracy is the exaltation of nonviolent conflict among relative equals.

Democratic government is both a means to the (sometimes mutually incompatible) goals of various individuals and groups, and an end in itself. It is a means because it instrumentally protects important freedoms — which are tokens not just of our ends but of the very possibility of pursuing the ends we choose. But precisely because democracy is the only known gateway to so much that we value, it can fairly be conceived as an end in itself. If it were something we prized only when we attained our personal goals, democracy would collapse.

Formally, democracy is in essence a kind (and a degree) of political equality among citizens vis-à-vis each other and their government. Political equality, in turn, assumes various forms, according to the type of interface between the individual and government. It embraces basic equality before the law; civil liberties, or the enumeration of specific freedoms against government, including rights to privacy, association, assembly, worship, etc.; and equality in making the law, through equal rights in relation to voting, advocacy, candidacy for office, and the like.

Questions such as who are to be counted as equals — children, teenagers, ex-felons, the mentally incompetent? — and in what ways and degrees they are deemed to be equal, are themselves key subjects of democratic debate. In every sense, a democracy is a self-regulating system. There may be lapses of integrity or accountability, but in the end it is the demos — the people — who do or fail to do the regulating.

If radical equality is an implausibly utopian (or dystopian) vision, then it remains to be determined just how much and what kinds of formal political equality we need or deserve. Democracy is both the venue and also, to some extent, the subject of such negotiation; it is in part a perpetual process of negotiation over the extent of democracy itself, and in part negotiation about other things, including capitalism and the power of the public over the private sector.

Thus, we may distinguish several basic egalitarian ideas within the concept of democracy. The most obvious one is the literal meaning of democracy, "rule of the people," through representative government. Another is the idea of civic or political equality — which is to say, basic equality among citizens in the forms relevant to such self-government. The civil rights movement in the United States was an effort to make American democracy more whole, to pursue the promise of political equality among all citizens that emerged from the Civil War and ensuing amendments to the Constitution.

Whereas journalism has to do with seeing, identifying, and understanding, the basic democratic concept of formal political equality among citizens turns on a seemingly quite different idea: an idea of fairness as public *blindness*: blindness to people's color, sex, religion, to their tastes or habits, hobbies, beliefs, education, profession, their personal experience or families, or to what they do in their bedrooms. Such blindness is essential to the rule of law and the formal equality on which democratic citizenship is based: the idea that a zone of conduct exists in which we are all treated alike, at least before our actions are taken into account.

Blindness of a kind is also a characteristic of how, in an ideal democracy, we treat one another: an equality of dignity or respect. This characteristic of democratic life and discourse for the most part cannot be written into the law, only into our hearts. Equal dignity, then, whereby we tolerate politically or morally irrelevant differences, such as those of behavior, opinion, or lifestyle, is a distinct form of democratic equality, and an important corollary of the others. Due to the vagaries of human nature, and because dignity is as much a cultural and psychological as a political phenomenon, this form of equality is inherently less precise and codifiable, and thus harder to institutionalize through law; it is always under attack. This is an inherent vulnerability of democracy, but perhaps not its greatest vulnerability. Against this background of democratic blindness, we must use journalism to see the world as it is.

Another concomitant of the concept of democracy is the idea of peaceful procedural and substantive change. Democracy is the alternative to rule by force; one of its salient features is the orderly and peaceful rotation of power. There is neither the instability of anarchic or semianarchic societies nor the static hyperstability of authoritarian or totalitarian regimes. Instead, there is stable, internalized change, predicated on free public discussion and debate, the gathering and sharing of information, and the airing of competing arguments and values. In other words:

As a mechanism for seeking or maintaining power, information is the chief alternative to force, and democracy is a way of organizing society around information rather than around force.

These democratic ideas did not spring up overnight, and they are not uniquely Western in origin. Amartya Sen and others have pointed out that early forms of proto-democracy were practiced in ancient Persia, in the Buddhist councils of India in the third century BCE, and elsewhere.[3] Various experiments in political equality existed not only in classical Greece and Rome (and perhaps also in prehistoric tribal communities) but also in the Norse *tings* (assemblies), in Venice and other late-Medieval Italian city-states, in England after the Magna Carta, and in Switzerland and the Low Countries well before the Protestant Reformation and the rise of modern capitalism. Iceland, under Norse influence, created a national assembly in 930 AD. Many of these societies also practiced slavery.[4] In the Western Hemisphere, early forms of democracy were practiced within the Iroquois confederation, with its constitution or "Great Law of Peace" and its Great Council, as well as in other native American tribes.[5]

In a wider historical context, democracy is not just a static state; it evolves over time, toward the ever-receding ideal of political equality, a slow, uneven ramping- and stepping-up process of expansion, inclusion, and redefinition, particularly of the idea of the citizen. American democracy failed to deal with its original sin of slavery and paid a horrific price; but it gradually came to embrace, in fitful expansions, female suffrage, direct election of the Senate, elimination of poll taxes and other barriers to civil rights, greater inclusion of minorities, and the lowering of the voting age to eighteen. Underlying it is the Framers' radical idea of government of, by, and for the people: not by corporations, unions, churches, or lobbyists, but by citizens.

What we have sketched thus far is no substitute for a thorough historical account of the rise of democracy. Nor is it a justification of republican government against its increasingly narrowing and nasty circle of rivals and critics; nor again is it comprehensive, inclusive of every democratic value, or every aspect of democratic government. It is simply a prelude, to which some further ideas will be added for perspective before we begin to explore more closely the connections of democracy to journalism and journalistic excellence. These further dimensions of the democratic idea will expand the platform on which we can consider that complex and intimate relationship.

3.   Ideology and Indeterminacy

Democracy in practice is a function of the interplay between two dimensions. One is a constant (or at least stable) legal and constitutional framework, a relatively fixed and static dimension based on political egalitarianism and its concomitants. The other dimension, a complex, wobbly, fluctuating, and dynamic variable, is the level of knowledge and participation on the part of citizens. It comes down, in the end, to the relationship between a semifixed framework of rules and human words and actions within that framework: to what and how much is known and done, and by how many citizens.

Within those channels, there is fluctuation and conflict around several axes. One of these is the relative latitude that citizens accord to the private and public spheres, respectively. We do not democratically determine what to eat for breakfast or what the weather will be; but we do decide the relative balance of the state and the market, the public and the private, and (what all of these relate to) of relative equality and inequality in the economic as well as the political sphere.

A concomitant feature of democracies is a range of ideological indeterminacy: uncertainty and unpredictability regarding policy outcomes, election outcomes, points or levels of consensus, the balance between private and public space, or the values that are promoted from time to time, as circumscribed by the law. Because such a system presents, broadly speaking, pervasive choices between more and less equality, agendas tend to compete in more or less binary fashion across what we call the left-right spectrum. It could just as well be up-down or blue-green, but the sheer persistence of issues of equality — in various forms, from the tax code to school vouchers to who pays for environmental damage or for health care — ensures the persistence of that continuum as the main fence across which democratic citizens argue.

Indeterminacy is thus intrinsic to democracy. It sustains the spectrum of opinion, giving people with divergent views and interests reasonable expectations that the system might at some point come to accommodate at least some of their goals. Such indeterminacy enables the political balance to shift peacefully while, ideally, the system itself remains ostensibly neutral.[6]

Two kinds of differences, which tend to go hand in hand but do not correlate perfectly, account for most of the substance of democratic debate: differences over economic status and interest, and differences over morality, as commonly seen in social issues such as abortion, gun control, school prayer, gay rights — major flashpoints in our time between the cultural antitheses of secular and religious views. It is because these issues overlap or parallel one another that we can talk, with just a bit of qualification, of a single left-right axis. (In fact, we could identify three or four distinct axes of ideological discord; but because they so closely parallel one another, it is easier to speak of a single axis.)

One of those parallel axes of left-right debate, alluded to earlier, is debate about the scope of democracy itself. While the left and right share a basic commitment to democratic discourse and law, the left's commitment to democratic principles is aspirationally broader, in keeping with its more egalitarian vision of a larger public sphere. Whereas conservatives, virtually by definition, seek to protect and extend the power of private enterprise, liberals favor not only more economic equality but more (and by their lights, better) democracy. This leads to a kind of "axis creep," a complicating factor in political debate; it means that we are often talking on two levels at once, and that while we may "agree to disagree," our differences include the scope of democracy itself.

There is a tinge of paradox in the fact that proponents of change toward the left — toward economic equality, the public sector, etc. — also tend to be proponents of extending democratic principles. It is assumed here that democracy needs no defense against its rivals; if any be necessary, it may be found elsewhere. But it cannot be assumed that everyone agrees on how much and what kinds of democracy are desirable. This is in fact, a highly contestable matter, although it is seldom contested openly or directly. It is not an issue that can or should rise above ideology or partisanship, that is, above firmly held and defensible value differences. It is one of those differences.

There may be wide support for basic democracy across the political spectrum; but there is not wide and equal support for extending democratic principles beyond their present bounds. (Here, especially, democracy itself is a class issue). At least two such areas of possible extension present themselves: first, economic democracy, for example, in the workplace; and second, movements to expand the public sphere or to protect it further against incursions by the private, such as through campaign finance reform. Put bluntly, extending democracy at the expense of market forces, commercial values, private wealth, etc., either in the political or in the economic arena, is almost universally favored on the left and disfavored on the right.

4. Economic Equality and Class

Power, like wealth, intelligence, and luck, can never be perfectly equalized. The more attainable ideal is a nation of maximally functional (engaged and informed) citizens, or what Christopher Lasch called an "attentive society." Such a society may opt for any balance between capitalism and socialism, between economic inequality and equality. That is a core ideological question. However, as Herbert J. Gans, among others, has noted, greater economic equality contributes to greater political equality.[7] The most advanced (informed, participatory, stable, and uncorrupt) democracies tend to be those with the least poverty and the strongest welfare states. Income inequality is both an economic and a political drain on society, especially as it becomes more extreme.

Inequality is an economic drain because it isolates an underclass of citizens from the reservoir of productive labor, consumption, investment, and taxation — to say nothing of the toll on individuals and families, and the cost to society in terms of containing the social pathologies that surround poverty. It is a political drain insofar as patterns of marginalization along demographic, ethnic, or income lines divide and weaken society as a whole. Inequalities of leisure time, and of human capital for civic activity, can be deleterious as well. Time is critical to functional citizenship, including news consumption, activism, and even the ability to vote. Thus, inequalities of wealth and leisure time do not stand alone; they amplify other political inequalities.[8]

Can either capitalism or socialism claim to be more consonant with self-government? The socialist ideal of radical economic equality is arguably more hospitable in theory to the democratic enterprise (despite the dismal history of undemocratic experiments in socialism's name). Calls for greater democracy seldom come from capitalists. The radical individualism, competitive behavior, and indifference to human needs that capitalism encourages are at least nominally hostile to democratic values such as communal problem-solving, consensus, and political equality. On the other hand, democracy is clearly compatible with socialist experiments; many highly democratic societies — across northern Europe, for example — are welfare states with important socialist elements. However, none of these points suggest that democracy itself is an inherently socialist idea, if that term is taken to mean an idea of economic egalitarianism. In reality we are all capitalists and socialists. Democracy is not in essence about one or the other polar form of society, but about continuously recalibrating the balance between them.

Moreover, democratic (political) equality is morally and politically antecedent to economic equality — just as it is antecedent to the individual economic freedoms we enjoy in the marketplace — because these are the very domains it regulates. In simple terms, political equality is the basis on which people decide what balance to strike between capitalist and socialist principles — between risk and security, inequality and equality, commonality and individualism, and so on. Elements of each are present in most societies. Street vendors are capitalistic, street cleaners are socialistic.

Neither does democracy inscribe a particular concept of class or economic hierarchy into society; at least in the abstract, it is class neutral. But we cannot avoid the fraught notion of class, because disparities of wealth, status, opportunity, etc., and the degree of mobility between levels, are among the central issues of democratic debate, subsuming many others. Democracy is in fact a venue where class issues are endlessly renegotiated: not for any final adjudication of competing values and interests, but for continually revised consensus.

Class is important and unavoidable because the division of power, status, and wealth are what politics is mainly about. The difference between democracies and other systems is the equal diffusion of formal political power, and thus the ability to talk and argue about — and actually change — social arrangements. This is the case even when class-sensitive issues are sublimated or obscured, as in the United States.

Various social myths propound the notion that class either does not exist, or does not matter because there is perfect mobility, or that even talking about class is somehow inappropriate or in bad taste — raising the specter of "class warfare." Such claims are politically self-serving (what better way to preserve something than to declare it out of bounds for debate), and somewhat reminiscent of antebellum defenses of slavery that referred to it indirectly as the southern "way of life."

Ideally, then, democracy is not an instrument of either capitalism or socialism per se, nor of any particular mixture of the two, but an end in itself — a vehicle for continual renegotiation of the balance or blending of those two archetypes.[9] The end of ideology is nowhere in sight. However, if democracies at their best are not biased toward change in any particular direction, they are (despite certain stabilizing structural features) biased toward the *possibility* of change, because that is what popular government is all about — the possibility of change (or affirmation of the status quo) and the equal power of citizens to effect or veto such change. The possibility of change is always a standing threat to the status quo.

Can there be too much democracy? Perhaps in some forms or contexts. Government by continual public referendum, for example, is no one's idea of a well-ordered democracy. The very idea of representative government is based on the understanding that every citizen cannot usefully participate directly in every decision. But while certain applications of the principles of political equality and majority rule are clearly not in the public interest (such as deciding by plebiscite whom the president should meet with in the Oval Office), other proposed expansions are at least debatable, and perhaps in the interests of some but not of others. Thus, to declare ideology's end, or to rule class issues out of bounds, is a disingenuous ploy that stunts democratic discourse itself.

5. Perfectibility and Complexity

Like virtually any set of values or norms, democracy implies an idea not of perfection, which is too much to ask, but of incremental perfectibility. It is not an ideal end-state but an ideal process, conditioned on political equality. As such, it is inseparable from the ideal of maximal mobility of information — the exchange of pertinent and well-produced facts and explanations.

The nub of the matter is that information is also an economic good. Democracy entails journalism; if democracy itself is perfectible, journalism is one of the things that perfects it. In other words, democracy does not just entail that there be some journalism; democracy depends on the quality of that journalism as well. In this sense, democracy is leveraged to the system and standards of journalism in a given society.

As we have already seen, there is a rather complicated relationship between the formal constitutive elements of democracy — constitution, laws, evolving legal rulings and decisions — and the informal and fluid elements that compose the level and breadth of citizens' knowledge and participation. Democracy, as G. Stuart Adam writes,[10] is the product of a complex set of institutions and cultural practices that include, minimally, the rule of law, a stable constitution, an independent judiciary, legislatures with representatives elected by citizens in regular and free elections, a universal adult suffrage, secure and basic rights, including freedom of expression and association, and a public that is informed and, in degrees, attentive to politics and the management of the state. ... Journalists, amongst others, provide information and thought on which consciousness of the state and its officers is formed. More broadly, journalists are prominently involved in the formation of social consciousness in the name of the public.

Given such complexity, there is no precise way of measuring the overall quality or quantity of a democracy, or determining how exactly such quality and quantity are interrelated. At best, we can identify and measure certain variables, such as rates of participation in voting. Knowledge is difficult to measure accurately and fully, let alone civic commitment, fellow-feeling, or ideological fervor.[11]

Along with education in general, the availability and quality of news production partially determines the overall level of civic knowledge. Hence the news, like formal education, book publishing, popular media, and anything else that contributes, however indirectly or indeterminately, to public information, is not just an adjunct to democratic life but an influence on it. The number of engaged citizens and the forms and extent of their participation and their knowledge — all are part of the complicated and delicate ecology of democratic culture. Calling democracy a "culture" is a way of identifying it as something that, because of the complexity of its sources, we cannot fully identify. Journalism is an essential part of that complex culture.

Democracies are complex in much the same way that other systems and organisms — such as the weather or the human body — are complex: they involve multiple identifiable parts, often interacting in obscure or unpredictable ways. They are complex, we might say, because of their concealed (or unobvious) inner movements, distinctions, and connections. These go well beyond the formal legal framework. They include the education system, the media system, the economy and business culture, the arts, folkways and conventions, religious practices and beliefs, and the overall social climate formed by all of these. All societies are complicated systems of interacting sectors and subsectors. In the democratic case, information — educational, journalistic, and otherwise — is the blood that provides oxygen to the civic brain.

Such systems can never create ideal citizens, much less improve upon human nature generally; citizenship is merely one role played (well or not well) by ordinary human beings. Laws or cultural values may help us to be better citizens, but people will always be different and diversely flawed, at least in each other's view. They will never be identical in their interests, energies, abilities, values, or in their personal and moral commitments to democratic life. Human beings, with the odd exception, will always be touched by depravity.

The dependence of democracy on the contingencies of citizenship, and citizenship's dependence in turn on education and journalism (among other things) are fatal to the idea that democracy itself can ever be finally achieved or perfected. It is always relative to, and limited by, the weaknesses and predations of human individuals and institutions. It is always less than it might be, or than we might imagine it to be. The software of human frailty and venality subverts the hardware of ideals imperfectly inscribed in codes and institutions.

Thus, democratic principles and institutions combine with economic, cultural, media, religious, and other modes of association and representation, to form the primordial goo out of which, for better or worse, democratic cultures are made. Some of these sectors are defined by clear logical distinctions, such as between the different social functions of law, money, cultural reproduction (arts and media), or faith. Sometimes they are pragmatic distinctions, useful because they marginally outweigh in importance the connections that they obscure. Each of them, in unquantifiable ways, promotes or impedes the ideal of political equality and helps to determine the overall level and quality of democratic life.[12]

Democracy and humanity are always works in progress, and so are democracy's two great propulsive forces, education and journalism. The various nemeses of citizenship — ignorance, apathy, corruption — can be combated and in some ways minimized; but, like crime and venality, they can never be wholly extirpated. This does not relieve us of the task of trying to improve our democracy's legal and constitutional hardware; if we cannot perfect our system of government, at least we can incrementally improve it. Levels of knowledge and participation are likewise imperfect but perfectible. Democracy is therefore an ideal that implies both different kinds and degrees of imperfection. Levels of knowledge and participation are among the most important and obvious democratic benchmarks, but they are not the only ones.[13]

In sum, even when constitutionally sound, a democracy is not a "machine that would go of itself," any more than an airplane can fly by itself if supplied with the proper manuals and checklists. It is more like a living organism, dependent upon the health and proper interaction of its moving as much as its static parts. It is a self-regulating system, but one that can perform at many levels of efficiency, and it is designed not to produce particular results, but to govern how they are derived.

6.   Democracy and Excellence

Although improvements to existing democracies are easy enough to postulate, an ideal democracy is harder to visualize. This is because democracy is a process for managing imperfection: for controlling and minimizing human conflict and for establishing baselines of fairness where perfect justice cannot be achieved. As such, it is at best a partial remedy for a host of flaws ingrained in the human condition. It can always be improved and optimized, but it has no "perfect" form, because in a perfect world it would not be necessary.

We can speak comparatively of better or worse examples, as when comparing the German or French system with the Russian or Mexican; but no political system can ever be perfectly democratic. As Winston Churchill famously quipped, "No one pretends that democracy is perfect or all-wise. Indeed, it has been said that democracy is the worst form of Government except for all those other forms that have been tried from time to time."[14]

At their best, democracies evolve, perfecting themselves slowly over time. Our very standards of democracy — and of citizenship in particular — have evolved from rather rudimentary beginnings. To suppose that this evolutionary process will continue is not radical or utopian; to accept democracy in any given form as the best of all possible worlds is to give up on the democratic ideal. A democracy cannot long remain static as the culture around it changes. The essential principles on which it runs do not change over time, but like a bicycle it must keep moving forward.

Democracies are not designed to promote human perfection or excellence in any particular sense. Ideally, they should enable us to be as free as possible, and to that end, good citizens; but they do not make us better writers or spouses. Popular government contributes to our overall well-being and to international peace, but it doesn't make us angels, and angels wouldn't need so complicated and clumsy a contrivance.[15]

Insofar as it is fundamentally egalitarian, democracy is at least nominally antithetical to excellence of other kinds; simply put, you can't have everything. By promoting political equality as a supreme principle, democracy trumps conventional notions of excellence when they conflict with that ideal. For example, we don't elect the ablest, smartest, most statesmanlike, or otherwise best political leaders; we simply elect the ones we like, democratically.[16]

Thus, far from ensuring other forms of excellence, democracies are in some ways engines of mediocrity. Majority rule does not optimize politically neutral values. In many cases, unless public ignorance is at code-red levels, there is no "right result," because the alternatives are essentially political. There is no higher moral principle to which one can appeal to determine which alternative is best. Another way of saying this is that democratic outcomes are "essentially contestable."[17]

Mussolini made the trains run on time, and Hitler built the Autobahn; postal systems, police departments, or other bureaucracies may be more efficient, on some neutral metric of efficiency, in undemocratic societies. We celebrate democratic equality not as the epitome or antithesis of excellence but as a morally superior *alternative* to excellence in any more conventional sense. In other words, political freedom and equality, as democratic values, are forms of moral excellence in the public sphere apart from anything else they may promote or inhibit.

Additional structural biases oppose excellence in the democratic process. For example, being governed by officials elected or appointed for fixed terms, democratic states are weighted toward the short term and against long-term vision or planning — something that the electronic media reinforce with their emphasis on the immediate, relative indifference to the past, and myopia vis–à–vis the future. Even the concept of representation has its problems. As Jacques Barzun has pointed out, "To please and do another's will is prostitution, but it remains the nub of the representative system." [18]

So democracy is not a recipe for excellence. But however imperfect or compromised by limiting conditions — including its own citizens — it is all we have, and it remains the task of democratic citizens to make the system work as well as possible given those limitations. It approaches perfection insofar as those citizens are truly equal (in terms of rights and in terms of their civic knowledge and engagement), and well-informed, regardless of how they govern themselves or whatever they may otherwise decide. What matters most is equal power in making those decisions, which in turn requires equal ability to access and to use the best possible information.

Democracies can disappoint their own ideals in innumerable ways. Executive incompetence and misbehavior, legislative gridlock and greed, corruption and cowardice, public ignorance, elections swayed by intolerance, impropriety, or wealth; judicial misconduct and incompetence, popular hysteria and prejudice: no undemocratic system has quite as many ways to go wrong. But then, undemocratic systems are illegitimate from the get-go and have no lofty ideals to betray.

Like democracy, our media system — less a product of intelligent design than a series of evolving, competing ways of dispersing commodified information — is not arranged to promote journalistic excellence as such.[19] Insofar as it is market-driven, it is not even a "system" in the narrower sense of a process designed to produce an outcome or range of outcomes (like a game or a factory assembly line), or an organism, like the human body. It is rather a set of more or less understood, conscious, and repeated processes, among identifiable institutions and individuals, with certain vaguely shared ideas, designed to make money by selling something (loosely or otherwise) called "news."

7. The Two Faces of Democracy and the Weak Slat

Democracy, as we noted earlier, has two interlocking dimensions. One is the more or less fixed conceptual and normative architecture of laws and rules. The object of that system is both to maximize political equality as an end in itself (a progressive, imperfectly achievable goal), and to ensure responsive, accountable law-making, and the orderly transfer of power between contending parties.

The other dimension is civil society — a fluid and ineffable culture that determines how those rules are applied, and with what tools, knowledge, attitudes, social practices, and institutions. The U.S. Constitution does not mention political parties, labor unions, interest groups, or public schools or universities; "the press" is notably mentioned in the First Amendment as an institution whose freedom the government may not, as a general principle, infringe. But all of these institutions are crucial to democratic life, and none does the Constitution ordain into existence.

This brings us to an important paradox — hardly the only one involving democratic government. Democratic systems, like baseball teams, may look good on paper but behave differently in reality. The constitutive rules are critical, but they are not the game. It takes an informed and active public to make them work. That is why the success of any democratic society depends partly on journalism — and not just the existence of such journalism, but its quality as well.

But what is to ensure that there be such excellence? How much is enough? Can the marketplace be trusted to provide it? Can the public even be relied upon to demand it in that marketplace or elsewhere? All of these questions reflect the paradox that democracies depend on good journalism, but cannot necessarily secure it for themselves. Democracies, as we have seen, are not designed to produce excellent results; they are designed, rather, to produce democratic results.

Journalistic excellence cannot be mandated, legislated, or manufactured. We rightly mistrust government as a primary source of information. Instead, we rely mainly on the marketplace. But as current news standards attest, the market is no guarantee of excellence either. The market is rather a continual inducement to pursue profit over excellence whenever they conflict — which is most of the time — by diminishing the news and diluting it with entertainment.

This is why TV networks have slashed their news budgets and reporting staffs, especially overseas, and why we do not have better reporting on areas of the world that matter to us, or better research to back it up; why media criticism is scant, especially in mainstream journalism; why there is little documentary journalism providing broader context for the news, or investigative reporting about inconvenient facts and patterns of behavior; why we continually need to worry about the "firewalls" between editorial and business functions of the media. It is also one reason so many people distrust the news media, regarding them collectively as an "it," an alien sector with its own agenda, distinct from that of informing citizens. Such distrust of the media (regarded and referred to as a singular phenomenon) is neither grammatical nor democratic.

It is impossible for all citizens to be fully informed, or equally informed, or even to stipulate precisely what we mean by "fully" and "equally." But this doesn't mean democracies can ignore the issues of public education and journalism. It means that in evaluating the quality or quantity of a democracy we are evaluating not just its legal framework but also the breadth and vibrancy of civil society in its public sphere, where citizens need to be educated and informed and motivated to act.

Education — including the form of education we call journalism or news — is indeed a slat under the bed of democracy, although as A. J. Liebling noted, the press is the "weak slat." This, in fact, is precisely where the question of journalistic excellence enters the picture. It is the idea of making that slat, and hence democracy, stronger. "Enlighten the people generally," said Thomas Jefferson, "and tyranny and oppressions of body and mind will vanish like evil spirits at the dawn of day." It may not be quite that easy; but democracy demands, or at least implores us to be, intelligent consumers of journalism. Democracy thus requires an essential ingredient that Jefferson understood and the Constitution foresaw but could not guarantee — good journalism. Even if we cannot touch it or measure it or open a spigot and watch it flow out, to the extent that we lack journalistic excellence, democracy itself is diminished.

Democratic culture is a complex ecosystem of rules and principles, formal and informal institutions, and moral and ideological values. An informed citizenry is part of that culture, which no constitution can mandate or ensure. Another part is a spirit of public tolerance and a desire to get along and reach consensus. That culture is fortified by at least a modicum of economic prosperity, mobility, and equality (and what is a modicum, anyway?) and by a robust civil society of private nonprofit organizations.[20]

Democracy even has a spiritual aspect: it brings people together, joining them in larger wholes, and in common enterprise for the wider good without regard to their other identities, a surrender of the self. We come together in agreement on certain principles, even as we differ on others. As such, it binds us in national communities (as religious, ethnic, or professional groupings do not) without diminishing those other affiliations. Journalism, as part of the democratic culture, is likewise a bonding process; James W. Carey called it the process of "forming a common mind," and "an imaginative construction of the social."[21]

The overall character or quality of a democracy is not something quantifiable. It is as much a matter of intensity, and a function of its civic life as well as of its laws. Thus, we cannot gauge how democratic a society is simply according to the size of its public or private sector. A better index (though not a final measure) is the vitality of its independent sector: that which is driven neither by government nor by the economic market. We shall return to this theme later on, as we proceed to explore the role of journalism in democracy, and the role of excellence in journalism. Governments are necessary, and so are free markets, so long as both are democratically controlled. But whereas the state and the market are equally capable of spreading light or darkness, of liberating or oppressing, nonprofit enterprise is more likely to be a pillar than a predator of democratic freedom.

Endnotes

1. B. Bagdikian, in Signal to Noise, pt. 3, "Remote Control."
2. In the case of the interstate highway system, one might question whether investment in other forms of transportation might have served democracy better. I use it as an example because historically it was the chosen path.

3. See Sen, A.., "Democracy and Its Global Roots," *The New Republic*, Oct. 2003; and "What's the Point of Democracy?" *Bulletin of the American Academy of Arts & Sciences* 57:3 (Spring 2004): 8–11.

4. See, for example, R. Dahl, On Democracy, Ch. 2.

5. See Charles C. Mann, "The Founding Sachems," *The New York Times* (July 4, 2005): A-13.

6. The American system is not perfectly neutral. The constitution originally tolerated slavery, even alloting electoral votes to the slave states that counted each slave as three fifths of a person, without giving slaves themselves citizenship of any kind. And the Senate and Electoral College skew the system to the right by granting disproportionate power to smaller states. But the possibility of changing laws, policies, and leaders constitutes the indeterminate core.

7. H. Gans, *Democracy and the News*, p. 116 and ff.

8. A salient example of this is the disenfranchisement of ex-felons in some states, an inconsistent, if not unconstitutional, pattern in which people who have served time for felony convictions are permanently barred from voting, even after completing their prison sentences: in effect, a powerful form of Jim Crow.

9. Class issues and differences per se clearly do not exhaust the range of possible and actual political differences. Moral, religious, ethnic, racial, professional, and other interests help to define us politically: differences that do not necessarily or neatly align with our class identities. But they do tend to so align. We might (too broadly) lump these into two opposing spheres: moral orthodoxy, which tends to be bound to religion, and moral heterodoxy, which tends to be secular and humanistic. Social issues such as gay rights, women's rights, abortion, capital punishment, separation of church and state, etc., tend to organize around this axis.

10. G. S. Adam, "The Education of Journalists," Journalism 2:3 (Dec. 2001): p. 316.

11. The qualitative variables of democracy would have to include not just the breadth and depth of citizen knowledge, based on both formal education and informal learning (such as journalism), and the breadth and extent of citizen participation, but also responsiveness of government, ease of consensus formation, fairness of voting systems, adequacy of civil liberties protections, etc.

12. Robert Dahl (On Democracy, p. 51) expressed a similar idea: "[D]emocracy could not long exist unless its citizens manage to create and maintain a supportive political culture, indeed a general culture supportive of [its] ideals and practices."

13. According to a study by the Institute for Democracy and Electoral Assistance (http://www.idea.int/vt/), the United States ranks 139th in the world in average voter turnout in national elections since 1945.
14. Churchill, Speech in the House of Commons, Nov. 11, 1947.
15. As A. Sen points out, the historical record is virtually devoid of instances of democratic states making war against other democratic states; in addition to which, "no substantial famine has ever occurred in any independent and democratic country with a relatively free press. We cannot find exceptions to this rule…" Sen notes that famine disappeared from India only after independence from Britain and the advent of multiparty democracy and a free press. (Sen, A., "What's the Point of Democracy?" Bulletin of the American Academy of Arts & Sciences 57:3 (Spring 2004): p. 10; "Democracy as a Universal Value," Journal of Democracy 10:3 (July 1999), pp. 7–8; and Sen, A., Development as Freedom.)
16. How far the United States is from approximating an ideal democratic state is a worthwhile question but too large to address here.
17. For further discussion see The Sound Bite Society, Ch. 4.
18. Barzun, "Is Democratic Theory for Export?" *Ethics & International Affairs*, Vol. 1 (1987): p. 68.
19. It might be quibbled here that if we define excellence in strictly relative terms, there is always journalistic excellence to be found. But if we accept such a limiting definition, there is little point in looking for higher forms of it or better ways to achieve more of it.
20. Leaving aside possible deficiencies in the Constitution, the United States would undoubtedly score highly on many of these benchmarks (as would many industrial societies). Three significant exceptions would be the persistence and extent of economic inequality, and the excessive power of economic and religious interests in the political system, respectively.
21. J. Carey, "Where Journalism Education Went Wrong," www.mtsu.edu/~masscom/seig96/carey.htm; pp. 8–9.

2

News and Democracy

> It is thanks to its claim of being able to offer the
> citizenry important and reliable knowledge that
> journalism justifies its position as a constitutive
> institution in a democratic society.
>
> — **Mats Ekström**[1]

I. Power and Knowledge

Democracy, as we have noted, consists of both constitutive
laws and instrumental institutions, both formal (government)
and informal (civil society). Some such institutions are educational and journalistic; but anything that enables people to
learn, communicate, or act politically, enriches democratic
culture. Popular government is not just a design but a social
force field; a kind of energy in continuous use and motion, the
energy of human actions and decisions.

What kinds of codified ideals make a society democratic
— or at least, relatively more democratic than another? The
rule of law and the legal establishment of certain formal rights
are clearly foundational. Democracies must secure equal rights
for all their citizens, and reasonable bases for citizenship itself.
But in practice it is the ability to actively exercise those rights
that expands the highly elastic democratic envelope; and the
exercise of such rights requires the availability to citizens of the
current information we loosely call "news."

Communication is central to all knowledge and action, and democracy is a quintessentially communicative process; it is about reaching decisions through conversation, as an alternative to shooting or pointing guns. The requisite knowledge may come from any source: personal conversation, rumor, gossip, e-mail, newsletters, or blogging. But ultimately it is institutional, based on education and journalism.[2] Transportation is another important factor, facilitating not just economic production but face-to-face communication, meetings and conferences, rallies, demonstrations, and other forms of public assembly.[3]

Power is a limited resource, of which most democratic citizens retain only a small amount. But knowledge and information are at least theoretically limitless and shareable. Knowing something doesn't normally prevent anyone else from knowing the same thing, or using such knowledge. And knowledge is also more difficult than power to define and categorize.

Even if we limit ourselves to knowledge that is important to democratic citizenship — call it civic knowledge — we are talking about something essentially vague and in constant flux. As events flow, issues, ideas, and personalities change, and over broader reaches of time, values evolve. Facts change — and which facts are important or relevant change as well. However much we may think we know, the ways in which knowledge is formed, distributed, and retained remain for the most part vague, complex, and even mysterious — and knowledge must be continually renewed by more, better, or fresher knowledge.

Multiple free agents can never be absolutely free. Citizens may be equally powerful in formal terms, such as in the right to vote; but if they are human they will also have different talents, capacities, drives, interests, values, thresholds of risk, etc. They will tend to conflict, as well as cooperate; to hurt as well as to help one another. Unequally shared knowledge translates to inequalities of power.

We aren't omniscient or omnipotent, and we cannot be "isocratically" (absolutely equally) informed in the same way as we are isocratic in our entitlement to vote or to enjoy other legal rights. We are naturally unequal and different in almost every conceivable way other than in our rights as citizens — including our appetites for, and abilities to process, knowledge of the world, whether it come from conversation, schooling, or the news media. Indeed, except in terms of our formal rights, we can never all be citizens in the same ways or degrees, just as we cannot know all of the same things or the same number of things.

Even the knowledge necessary for citizenship, or civic knowledge, can be specified only vaguely. Ideally, all citizens should have at least rudimentary understanding of how a democratic political system works, the principles on which it is based, how they may potentially function within it and be affected by it, what the important issues are, and how those issues change over time. Because most knowledge of events and issues is filtered through the media, citizens should have a sense of how the media report and affect — and to a great extent, select — those issues and events for public attention.

Representative government also entails the delegation of knowledge and power to elected and appointed officials. Democracies, like all societies, include many who are too young, too old, too sick, too apathetic or cynical, or too impaired to be active citizens. Nevertheless, functional citizens need enough good information to make informed judgments (if and as they so choose); as Col. Rainborough said in the Putney Debates in seventeenth-century England, "The smallest he that live in England hath a life to live as the biggest he." For this reason if no other, it behooves the democratic citizen to know not only how the political system works, but how the media reflect and explain it. And the higher the quality of news, the better for democracy.

2.   Democracy and Media: Separated at Birth?

How then do the media — in narrower terms, the news media, but more broadly, all forms of public information and entertainment — figure within the foundations of democracy? In what sense do democratic discourse and institutions involve those media? We can identify several obvious ways.

Most obviously, popular government depends on the flow of information to and among the public, much as the human body depends on the circulation of blood to carry oxygen to its organs. That is why freedom of speech and expression are predicates of any democracy, and are thus privileged in the First Amendment.

Second, the media are also in most cases in business, and as such are subject to the same debates about private enterprise and government regulation for the public good as are other industries. Media organizations exist in the economic as well as in the legal and political realms; they pay taxes, file documents with government agencies, hold broadcast licenses or have joint operating agreements, hire and fire employees, often issue stock for sale to the public, and otherwise function as for-profit corporations. Like any such commercial enterprise, they are subject to the rule of law, including laws specifically governing the media.

If democracies require free and uncensored media, it is not quite as clear that commercial media depend reciprocally on democracy. Private media enterprises survive under most nontotalitarian dictatorships as long as they don't offend the powers that be and are willing to submit to censorship. But at the very least they depend on freedom to disseminate information; and ordinary citizens and public officials alike depend on the information they sell.

Third, the media collectively enjoy, almost by definition, a near monopoly on current public information. With certain exceptions, such as town meetings, most important political debates require the media as a venue for publication or broadcast. Media companies are not the only conduits of information or loci of debate; as private individuals we can still get up on a soap box and speak to whoever will remain within earshot, or maintain our own Web sites (with the help of corporate service providers). But for better or worse, without institutional media there would be a huge vacuum where our debates take place, and a far narrower information stream.

Fourth, just as we delegate powers to elected officials in a democracy, we delegate to the news media the function of deciding what information is important enough to be disseminated — what should count as civic knowledge, among other things. They — not the government or elected officials or ordinary citizens — are the primary gatekeepers of what is discussed and debated.

Fifth (a subfunction of the gate-keeping role), the media are also watchdogs, democracy's trip wire for abuse or misbehavior. The watchdog function is partly a check on the natural, and sometimes corrupt, penchant of public officials and institutions for secrecy. Supplementing the government's limited ability to check itself through the separation of powers, and the public's similarly limited ability to check the powers of government without publicly shared knowledge, the watchdog function is a critical part of the media's general role as conduit of information — the part that tends to lead to more immediate change. Robert W. McChesney puts it concisely:

> Within democratic theory, there are two indispensable functions that journalism must serve in a self-governing society. First, the media system must provide a rigorous accounting of people in power and people who want to be in power, in both the public and private sector. This is known as the watchdog role. Second, the media system must provide reliable information and a wide range of informed opinions on the important social and political issues of the day. No single medium can or should be expected to provide all of this; but the media system as a whole should provide easy access to this for all citizens. Unless a society has journalism that approaches these goals, it can scarcely be a self-governing society of political equals.[4]

In sum, the general democratic responsibilities of news media include: informing people on factual matters relevant to their civic duties; explaining and clarifying those facts by putting them in context; providing a check against abuses of power by probing behind the curtains of government, commerce, and other public enterprise; and providing a venue for discussion and debate.

The news does not just report about Washington or our neighborhood block association. It also informs us in other ways, as economic and cultural citizens, entertainment audiences, sports fans, puzzle enthusiasts, and as victims of the same weather. Journalism may help us to decide where to eat, what movies to see, what books to read, where to shop, how to invest our money, or how to fritter it away playing the lottery. At its best it provides deeper insights, alerts us to problems, prepares us for change, or poses alternatives for such change. There may even be useful information in the advertisements — at least in the classifieds. Here, however, we are mainly interested in its democratic functions. We are not looking at democracy through journalism's lens, but at journalism through democracy's lens.

3.   The Need to Know, and the World without News

Democracy is based on input by citizens. It does not generate power without fuel; simply having a constitution in a vacuum-sealed case is not enough. Such a system of government will not flow all over us, endowing us equally with the blessings of liberty; nor will it function as well if some participate and others do not.[5] We need the news in order to be full citizens, and because we are naturally curious about, and often affected by, all sorts of forces beyond our immediate control: political, economic, cultural, technological, natural.

Why do democratic societies need good information? And what *is* good information? The first question is much easier to answer than the second; the reason, perhaps, is that while both democracy and information (language, images, symbols) are human systems, democracy is a relatively closed system, based on a finite, if changeable, set of rules, whereas communication is more open and indeterminate.

So while we are not ready to say what constitutes good or bad journalism (we will take a stab at that in the next chapter), we can say that democracies need the best journalism they can get (or at least, the best that citizens are capable of consuming). Better information, *ipso facto,* makes for better citizenship. This is not a truism, and it can be understood in two ways. First, good journalism promotes citizenship, other things being equal; and second, we must define and measure the quality of journalism mainly in terms of its civic utility.

Better journalism, along with its long-lost twin, better education, is no panacea. Democracy still depends on people, including nonjournalists. But quality journalism is pivotal to the quality of democratic culture. It would be just as necessary even if all of the worst flaws of the legal-constitutional system were corrected.[6]

Fully engaged citizens need not engorge themselves with the best news they can find on a daily or hourly basis. There is more to life than that. So why couldn't one be an attentive citizen simply by catching up once in a while, however one pleased — say, by reading books or watching documentaries? To some extent, of course, one can. No recipe for citizenship calls for a fixed amount of civic knowledge (if we can even speak of knowledge as coming in "amounts") or a particular news diet. There is no one path to civic knowledge, much less to citizenship. The extent of one's daily appetite for the stuff is not the ultimate measure of civic wisdom or commitment.

Let's qualify that just a bit. News doesn't break when we feel like hearing about it; and its importance is not limited to its personal importance to us. Human events on a larger scale have their own rhythm, and following that rhythm is not without its benefits. The sheer attention to events is a form of citizenship in itself, keeping us civically alert. Even if the news is not always enriching, and *War and Peace* beckons from the bookshelf, there is always some new information to be learned.

Furthermore, news does not simply fill gaps in our knowledge or satisfy our curiosity. We also need good daily journalism to choke off the competing forms of information, such as rumor or propaganda, which would fill the information vacuum. News keeps those lesser alternatives at bay. It chokes off some of the weeds that grow between our foundational knowledge and our daily awareness of the here and now. In its continuity, especially with the advent of cable TV and the Internet, news has the potential to seal the lining of public opinion against misinformation, manipulation, and flimflam.

It is not a stretch to say that the need for news has a spiritual quality, like democracy itself: a desire to connect with others and with society, to be "in the know" on particular subjects or to satisfy general curiosity, to be conversant with one's peers, to *connect*. Spirituality is about connection and integration of the self into larger wholes, as is information. Sometimes they converge.

Looking at the darker side, imagine what might happen if a democracy were to decline into ignorance and apathy. It would still function on some level — all the outward trappings, the "hardware," would remain — and it might even function happily for some of its citizens (or quasi-citizens). Would the nation run off the rails? Not entirely, or right away; it would first experience a kind of spiritual decay and a general erosion of democratic values; a loss of cohesion among its citizens, and a loss of faith and interest in democratic life as such.

Such a democratic culture could well become lazy, immature, fearful, and over-commercialized. This could lead to disputed elections, or blooms of corruption and venality in high places; its elected leaders might fight reckless wars, and mistreat enemies in captivity in defiance of its own traditions and international law; use foreign threats to scare the public for political gain; encroach on civil liberties; behave callously toward citizens in distress after natural disasters. Almost certainly, such a lapsed democratic society would be marked by increasing bitterness and division at home, and severe erosion of its reputation abroad. So let's not go there.

As for the role of journalism, one can imagine a world without news altogether, or at least without news as we know it. It does not conjure up a happy picture. Under communism, party oligarchies dispensed a limited, controlled, and monopolized flow of information pertaining to actual events — propaganda mixed with the odd fact. Propaganda is likewise dispensed as a means of social control in Orwell's *1984*. Statist regimes are never indifferent to information; they are compelled either to produce propaganda, or to tolerate and censor something approximating journalism or propaganda in the guise of journalism.

Information supplied by the state in such real and imagined societies hardly qualifies as what we care to call news — a regular flow of topical information, describing and explaining actual events, and intended chiefly to inform rather than to intimidate, control, influence, or persuade. (Bingo! News is a moral category, a type of information superior to those others; how could news be integral to democracy and not have some moral cast?) Even in freer early societies there was not a lot of what we call news until the eighteenth century, long after the invention of the printing press; news evolved along with those societies.

We might also wonder, in passing, what sort of democracy there could be without public schools or universities. Our own began with none of the former and a mere handful of the latter. Places of learning are not foreordained or inscribed in the Constitution. Yet few would deny that they have vastly strengthened American democracy, increasing both the number of functional citizens and the level of their functioning.

The provision of news, like education, is a quintessentially democratic aspiration. In the absence of independent news, there is not some innocent, prelapsarian state of nature, but rather a void filled by rumor and opinion. The theorist of that state is not Thomas Hobbes but Joseph Goebbels.

This is not to say that news is limited to democratic societies; since the advent of mass journalism in the nineteenth century, all sorts of nasty regimes have felt compelled to produce, tolerate, or censor but not wholly suppress, something approximating journalism. Any society requires a flow of information or propaganda, brokered by mediating institutions within or beyond the state's control. So a world without news is possible, but not a world without public communication of some kind.

It is harder to imagine a society in which there is no public *demand* for news; here we are edging closer to science fiction, perhaps along the lines of *The Stepford Wives.* Most people are curious about the world outside their immediate experience; we are curious by nature, in a slightly prurient way, about other people's lives. If nothing else, their troubles and foibles confirm that we are not alone in our imperfection.

To be sure, some people are more interested in the news than others. Some consume news for more civic-minded reasons; some have more ability to process news or better access to it. We are not talking about a human need on a par with food or shelter. But mankind is for the most part naturally social and inquisitive, driven at once toward community and toward knowledge of that community (as well as toward isolation of the self and one's own communities from contaminating others). Knowledge is, among other things, a survival strategy, whether in the desert or rainforest or in the boardroom or union hall. Sometimes we are curious even about other communities and societies.

In a dictatorship, we wouldn't need news for political action and choice. But there still might be vestigial curiosity about the world: human interest stories, weather, sports, and the like. If there were no citizenship, we might still want to know what policies were being pursued by our rulers. Even if we didn't need to know these things, we would think up other things to be curious about. So it is hard to hypothesize our way out of a need for news. Hermits may neither want nor need news, but to the extent that we are not hermits, we tend to want some form of it. And a democracy of hermits is not a pretty picture.

What is hardest of all to imagine is a democracy without news — indeed, it is a contradiction in terms. Democracies cannot function without citizens, and citizens cannot function without civic knowledge. Even if democracy meant respect only for certain basic human rights and civil liberties, it would require the ability to communicate freely. But if democracy means representative government and political equality among active citizens, it cannot subsist in any meaningful form without journalism.

A democracy without news is thus an impossibility. If there were an alternative route to civic knowledge, such as by injection or implant, so much the better. But thus far at least, the conduct of democracy still requires journalism. And therein lies the central paradox alluded to in Chapter 1:

Democracies need news, but cannot guarantee news.

In the United States, only the marketplace (with which our democratic system is loath to interfere) guarantees that we have any news at all, let alone good news. We are at the mercy of the market for journalistic excellence, as well as being limited by the availability of talent, the cultural consensus and market determination of how such talent should be used, and so forth. At the very least, this is a troubling paradox for those who recognize moral values in journalism and democracy that transcend concerns for wealth, fame, or power.

4.   The Watchdog's Bark

Investigative journalism, insofar as it is a discrete genre of reporting, plays a special role in democratic life. It is democracy's alarm system, variously revealing what urgently needs to be known, what is harder to know, what someone in power doesn't want known, and what should have been known all along. Investigative journalism is thus essentially revelatory — a combination of digging and barking to show what has been dug up — bringing to light facts that were hitherto concealed at a cost to the public interest.

If anyone is paying attention, the revelation typically triggers a democratic change or adjustment: policy or personnel changes, criminal prosecution, legislation, or heightened public consciousness leading to altered public behavior as citizens or consumers. It is essentially a rear-guard action against the breach of public trust, intended to correct flaws in the democratic fabric. Thus, while ordinary journalism is democracy's informational fuel, investigative journalism and its overlapping watch-dog function are not just propulsive but also reparative, restoring public accountability about public matters. (What is a public matter? It's a matter that affects the public, and often we know it when we see it, but that still leaves open to debate the definitions of *matter, affect,* and *public*).

Investigative journalism requires the construction of narratives not unlike those of daily hard news, but on a larger scale of time and significance — the revelation of trends or patterns over a longer span. It also involves greater factual detail, such as that emerging from the close examination of public records:

> The epistemology of the investigative journalist [write J. S. Ettema and T. L. Glasser] … distinguishes itself from that of the daily journalist in three important ways. First, the investigative reporter accommodates a variety of types of fact, including facts dismissed by the daily reporter as bureaucratically incredible. Second, the investigative reporter assesses the relative quality of facts, an essentially rational — even if imprecise — process from which facts emerge as more credible or less credible. And third, the investigative reporter seeks to justify the larger truth of the story, a truth often greater than the sum of the story's facts.[7]

Investigative journalism does not require a license; all solid, independent public-affairs reporting is in some sense investigative. It may mitigate the failures of public figures, law enforcement, and routine or mediocre journalism alike, by bringing to light facts that should have been exposed routinely — or that good journalism might have prevented from becoming fact in the first place. Solid reporting, investigative or otherwise, is always on the lookout for such revelations. It thus fills a critical watchdog function — to "find out what the bastards are up to and tell the world."[8]

In revealing flaws in the legal-political system, the market, or other aspects of civic life, the investigative journalist is less like a teacher than a pathologist, looking for cancer cells in biopsies of the body politic.[9] The analogy falters in cases where public knowledge of the condition is a sufficient cure; where public opinion is the main thing that needs adjustment. Mere knowledge of the presence of cancer is not a cure, but it is a first step.

Investigative journalism often involves verifying suggested facts or tips, public knowledge of which would have political or legal consequences. That knowledge, once established and publicized, may directly influence public opinion or political behavior; in the extreme, the result might be a public figure's resignation, a criminal prosecution or indictment, policy change, new laws or regulations, embarrassment or damaged reputations, or, in the case of a company, a change in management, loss of market share, or a decline in stock price. Above all, changes in law, leadership, or consumer knowledge and behavior are the outcomes of true investigative reporting.

How good is a news organization? Find out how many investigative series it has featured that questioned powers that be or led to change. It is the role of news organizations and journalists to be skeptical and contrarian, but not cynical, on the public's behalf; to question authority, but not to applaud or indict at every turn; and to report in ways that lead to constructive change, but as a catalyst and not a change agent. How do we identify journalistic excellence? Show me the courage.

In an ideal world, perhaps, there would be no need for investigative journalism; the transparency of public life would obviate the need for exposés because there would be nothing to expose. Any public malfeasance would be deterred by media vigilance, alert civil servants, or law enforcement. With everything so on the up-and-up, journalists would have nothing to investigate.

For that matter, in a perfect world we wouldn't need ordinary journalism either, or government of any kind, including police, firefighters, meter maids, or tax collectors. But on this planet they are useful. More than that, investigative journalists, like teachers, are true guardians of democracy, unlike elected officials who are easily replaceable, and who prattle about "public service" as if getting elected to office were a noble sacrifice.

5. The Necessity and Contingency of News

If journalism, investigative or otherwise, is so important, where does it come from? What ensures that there is even a trickle of news — much less that it be of high quality? Nothing in the U.S. Constitution guarantees that there be news, let alone high-quality news. The First Amendment aims to ensure that laws limiting freedom of the press are not passed, and that voices are not peremptorily censored or silenced, but it does not say that news must be gathered and disseminated, or that a full, truthful, and diverse flow of information be provided to the people. Nor is it written anywhere that journalists should view their jobs as relevant — much less crucial — to the democratic process. Thomas Jefferson might have lost some sleep over it, but the brutal fact is: *You cannot legislate journalism or excellence, let alone journalistic excellence.*

Of course, an economic (as well as a political) demand for news exists, which is one reason why we have it; there are people who know that we want news and are willing to take our money. But that doesn't answer the hypothetical question: what if all journalists just packed up and went home? What if they all abandoned the pretense of serving democracy, and confined their labors to documenting the love lives and love children of celebrities?

There are two basic answers to that question, and they comprise two of the main themes of this book. First the easy one: nothing stops democracies from overdosing on mediocrity, commercial or otherwise — nothing at all. Various forms of human enterprise, in the extreme, become inimical to democratic life: market orthodoxy, religious or moral orthodoxy, ignorance, poverty, militarism. Democracies, for better or worse, are capable of tolerating all such excesses, and deteriorating, without either reforming or yielding to authoritarian alternatives. We can survive a lot of mediocrity without finding (or even looking for) a fix.

The second answer is that such a fix, while difficult, is not impossible. Sick or dysfunctional democratic systems can self-medicate, so to speak, if their citizen-patients are sufficiently informed and motivated. Democracies are frameworks for change; the democratic spirit is always willing, even when the body politic is not. How many engaged citizens does it take to screw in a lightbulb? Maybe quite a few.

As unlikely as it may be that a democratic society should end up having no news, or no high-quality news, the fact remains that this crucial democratic function is mostly outsourced. It is left by default to the private sector, and the energy, talent, and integrity of the people and institutions within it. Children are required by law to attend school, but no one is required to read newspapers or watch TV news or check out news Web sites on the Internet. If every journalist — good, bad or indifferent — suddenly gave up journalism in order to stay home or sell Tupperware, no laws would be broken. But when was the last time you relied on the United States Information Agency for your news? (And it is hardly the worst source available.) This outsourcing of one of democracy's most basic needs is a central democratic paradox.

6. The Contingency of Excellence

If journalism is contingent in democratic regimes, rather than foreordained, then journalistic excellence is contingent in an even stronger sense, because it is even harder to secure, and more dependent on forces that are largely independent of those regimes.[10] Good reporting, however we define it, cannot be taken for granted unless we relativize (and thus severely limit) the very notion of excellence, in effect grading on a curve.

It is not legal or natural necessity that prevents news organizations from going out of business, focusing on fluff or fiction, or filling their editorial ranks with illiterates or mental patients. It is the marketplace, along with the values of journalism: traditions, canons of professionalism, devotion to civic ideals. The same is true for other professions, of course; dentists exist only because of the public need for them, which seems reason enough, even if defined in economic terms; but then, democracy as such does not require dentists either.

The point isn't trivial, however. Whatever it is that prevents journalism from disappearing, and whatever prevents mediocrity from blooming like algae in a stagnant pond, it is culturally determined. And this tells us something very basic about democracies, which applies beyond the media but is signally important in the media context; democracies depend for their overall health on factors that are beyond the reach of law or economics, and are determined by a much broader and more complex culture.

If democracies didn't need informed citizens — or if there were some better form of government requiring no human input whatsoever — we wouldn't need journalism either (at least not for citizenship — the crossword puzzles might stay), and politics would look very different than it does now. But, given that democracies are flawed, and based on popular input, journalism is needed to inform decisions and catalyze change.

There are practical limits, of course, to what we can expect in the way of journalistic excellence; it can't *all* be great. But that doesn't exempt us from the responsibility of asking how it might be made better, what constitutes "better" (or good enough), and what the relation of such quality is to democracy. The whole business of identifying excellence (for example, by awarding prizes or allotting praise) is based on the implicit hope of raising the overall level, and the possibility of coming marginally closer to ideals.

In similar fashion, I have suggested that part of the business of any democracy is to improve itself, to become *more* democratic. It is a system that naturally seeks to perfect itself, in constant struggle with competing forces, whether ideological, religious, military, or economic. (While circumstances may dictate which struggle is more important, it is also the business of democracies to avoid becoming *less* democratic.) And the quality of a democracy is partly a function of the quality of its journalism. It is therefore the business of democratic citizens to try to improve the quality of their journalism. Excellence in journalism, as in democracy generally, can be neither wholly relative nor absolute. It is an envelope that we must continually push.

Endnotes

1. M. Ekström, "Epistemologies of TV Journalism: A Theoretical Framework," *Critical Studies in Mass Communication* 3:3 (2002), p. 260.
2. The differences between news and education as rubrics of communication are fairly obvious. Education is essentially foundational, formal, involuntary (in the lower grades) and more strictly knowledge- and skill-oriented.

News is more immediate, voluntary, and adult-oriented, and less formal in the sense of combining commercial and civic functions, and thus blending information and entertainment, the balance varying according to the medium, intended audience, economic structure, etc.

3. Although unquantifiable, the post-World War II achievements furthering American democracy include not only the GI Bill and the Civil Rights Movement, and for those with access the Internet, but also the interstate highway system and the national air transport system, like the rail system before it.

4. R.W. McChesney, "Journalism, Democracy, ... and Class Struggle," *Monthly Review* Vol. 52, No. 6 (Nov. 2000): pp. 2–3.

5. There is a lively debate among political scientists and others about the importance of higher levels of citizen engagement in the smooth functioning of a democracy. Arguably, higher levels of participation and information are not instrumental to greater democracy, but rather constitute greater democracy.

6. In the American case, two such flaws seem to me glaring: the lack of insularity of the democratic process from the corruption of private wealth, through lobbying and campaign finance; and the lack of a general Constitutional right to privacy.

7. J.S. Ettema, & T.L. Glasser, "On the Epistemology of Investigative Journalism," *Communication* Vol. 8 (1985): 183-206; p. 202.

8. Simon Jenkins, quoted in K. Sanders, *Ethics & Journalism*, p. 8.

9. In this context, the market may be considered a subset of the democratic system, insofar as it is regulated by the state or insofar as market failures or undesirable effects (e.g., on consumers, workers, communities, etc.) may be grounds for regulation. One of the first principles of democracy is that markets must serve democratic states, not vice versa.

10. In a sense this is logically true, insofar as all journalism cannot be deemed "excellent" or the term loses its semantic utility. Excellence must always be applied to a subset of the field of reference. (We may deem all baseball players "excellent" only by widening that field and comparing them to, say, minor league or semi-pro players.) In an equally trivial logical sense, there is always some excellence in any particular field of human evaluation, because that is how we differentiate the best from everything else. But we are talking here about the practical problem of maximizing excellence.

3

The Shape of Journalistic Excellence

Every generation creates its own journalism.
— **Bill Kovach and Tom Rosenstiel,**
The Elements of Journalism

I. The Nature of Excellence

At first glance, the idea of excellence seems like something of a cipher. It is a concept of high or maximum quality or value in connection to some type of performance or achievement; and we tend to generalize it over time. We may find examples of excellence, but it is also a kind of practice or consistency of achievement. Excellence represents a form of maximized value, but no single thing, process, quality, or relationship defines it; in each sphere, the standards are different. Thus, excellence in cooking has little or nothing to do with excellence in acting or chess-playing, except that each requires some combination of talent and effort.

The definitional boundaries of journalism, and of journalistic excellence, are less clear than those of cooking or chess. In journalism, as in acting (and to a lesser extent perhaps in cooking or chess) we cannot simply equate excellence with popularity or success. Often they coincide, but sometimes they do not.

Another question to consider is in what sense excellence is relative. Is it merely a linguistic prize, identifying the best we can find, or can it be propagated up to a point — and if so, to what point? Could excellence maintain its meaning in the absence of contrasting average, mediocre, and bad things? Could all food be excellent, or all chess players? Could all works of art, at some far future date, be masterpieces?

Practically speaking, it seems unlikely that lesser artists would retire, or that experts and public taste in general would come to deem all works of art (or all food) to be equally great. We would still need mediocre art, if only to fill the walls of motel rooms. How is journalism different — and are there journalistic equivalents of motel rooms? Like teachers, artists, and motel decorators, journalists can always try to do better, and we have general notions of what "better" means. The very absence of clear, objective standards of news production would seem to leave room for the continual pursuit of better results.

Strictly speaking, neither logic nor experience prevents excellence in any human endeavor — art, journalism, the pursuit of world peace — from simply busting out all over. Logic merely safeguards our ideas from contradiction, circularity, and dead ends; experience is a muddy and complicated thing, which is exactly why notions like excellence are useful. As long as people and institutions vary in their abilities, productivity, resources, interests, luck, etc., there is room for improvement in most arenas of human enterprise. There is room to argue about appropriate standards of achievement and useful, if uncertain or contestable, standards that define what constitutes the good, the bad, and the ugly.

So let us begin with a few safe but nontrivial assumptions. First, excellence is a meaningful and useful concept in the world as we know it — a world in which graded ascriptions of value make sense. Second, excellence is at least somewhat relative; all journalism cannot be excellent because all human beings and institutions and societies are not identical. If everything were excellent, the term would lose its meaning; mediocrity (or something worse) must anchor the opposite end of the evaluative scale. Excellence must be relative at least in the sense of distinguishing the best from the rest, as long as there is a "rest" to distinguish. In this sense it is plainly a ranking concept.

Third, excellence cannot be entirely relative, or there would be nothing we could do to promote it; we could merely identify the best. And it is not a fixed quantity; if we cannot simply manufacture more excellence, at least we can coax it into being now and then, or encourage the replication of existing specimens, if only to avoid sliding the other way. That is what makes it an ideal worth pursuing, and not just worth identifying.

Fourth, in most contexts (other than multiple-choice tests) excellence cannot be equated with the more elusive and extravagant (but nevertheless useful) notion of perfection. This is especially true in areas that are more difficult to quantify and evaluate, such as the diffusion of information or knowledge; it may still be possible to mow a lawn more or less perfectly. Excellence, rather, identifies attainable goals — the nearest we can reasonably aspire to perfection or expect it of others. It is about evaluating and educating — teaching and promoting the best — and not just about grading on a curve, although life does have some curves that need grading. To judge is to teach; we are not gods, and gods do not need education or journalism.

We commonly use the term *excellence* without pondering its intrinsic vagueness. No one hears the phrase *journalistic excellence* and immediately thinks: What the hell does *that* mean? We know it is a judgment, distinguishing the best journalism from the rest, and that it is probably discriminating on the basis of commonly understood and shared values. (That is not to say we always agree on what excellent journalism is.) Such vagueness is tolerable for several reasons. A degree of vagueness is endemic to all human communication, yet somehow we manage to communicate. Also, there is broad general agreement about how the term *excellence* is and is not used; and the semantic implications of the context in which we use the term (such as journalism, teaching, or cooking) further alleviate vagueness and enable us to use it successfully.

Thus, without assigning it any specific content, we can say that excellence is about value, that it is partly relative, and that it pertains to activities sufficiently common and important that higher forms of achievement are widely if not universally recognized. Amazon tribes may not value the form of excellence recognized and celebrated by the Emmy Awards, but that does not denigrate either their judgment or the awards.

2. Excellence, Perfection, and Culture

A natural complement of excellence is the aforementioned ideal of perfection; there cannot be a sense of what is better without at least a vague notion of what is best, if only in imagination. But some ideals are more specifiable or more attainable than others. In the unscientific world of journalism, there is no single Archimedean Point or Holy Grail (or maybe there is just one, along with some reliable polestars). And little, if any, journalism could be called "perfect" without embarrassment; there are only discernible grades of excellence and mediocrity.

The same is true for most human endeavors. We do not normally speak of excellence in smoking, peeling carrots, or dog-walking, but any of these activities can be done well or botched. There are reasonably clear benchmarks for adequacy or success. Some things can be done well in more than one way, and there is room to differ about which way is best; there are also many ways to screw up. There are not many ways to land a plane safely, but many ways to crash. Thus, we do not see headlines that read "Zero Killed as Plane Lands Safely."

Excellence more often refers to the dependable repetition of mundane but difficult activities — teaching, parenting, cabinet-making, reporting — practiced successfully over time. Even hacks do not do these things by rote; they require knowledge, imagination, judgment, a sense of proportion or scale, and a feel for one's audience. This dependability over time, and the ephemeral but crucial bond of trust it implies between journalist and audience, are cited by the French journalist Bernard Poulet in a conversation about *Le Monde* and journalistic excellence:

> *Le Monde* convinced itself that great journalism was a steady diet of Watergates and exposés. But, really, what is a great newspaper? It isn't one that has exposés and revelations every day. It is one that has credibility, competence, and good writing. It is the daily drip of trustworthy competence and reliability that made the old *Le Monde* great. If we admire the *Financial Times* or the *Economist* or the *New York Times* or the *Guardian*, it isn't because they break story after story … [i]t is because day in, day out, week in, week

out, they promise a level of intelligent commentary and credible information.[1]

One problem in developing a fuller model of journalistic excellence is the impossibility of gauging the actual *effects* of journalism on audiences. Such effects must surely exist or journalism would be pointless; but they tend to be invisible, imponderable, and unquantifiable. Most kinds of knowledge can only be measured by either very specific or very general metrics; and it is even harder to link such knowledge, as effect, to particular causes. At best we can make rough comparisons. But our language has a wisdom of its own. *Excellence* and *perfection* are both useful terms, identifying (and serving as models of) the best possible and the best imaginable.

So what does excellence mean in the context of journalism? What are the appropriate standards of journalistic excellence, where do they come from, and how do they relate to democracy? How can such standards be promoted, and how can we get the best possible news? This chapter outlines some answers to those questions, and later chapters will explore them further.

First a reminder: the pursuit of journalistic excellence is an essential part of the practice of democracy. No information, no democracy; no good information, no good democracy (or not much). These are axioms of our inquiry. As noted earlier, democracy is no guarantee of excellent leadership (or, for that matter, of excellent citizenship). That is where the human element — and the cultural element of groups, institutions, and mass society — come into play.

Even great journalism is pointless if no one consumes it, like a proverbial tree falling in the forest, or a brilliant lecture in an empty classroom. Likewise, even informed citizenship can be taken to extremes. Citizenship isn't everything; sometimes it is okay just to watch TV or play with your cat. But journalistic excellence makes for better-informed citizens. It guarantees nothing, but makes more things possible through informed action.

One thing about journalistic excellence is clear, if not self-evident: there is no single defining archetype, just as no teacher, curriculum, or school can constitute or define a great education. No journalistic specimen at any level — no story, format, technique, organization, or individual journalist — can be exclusively equated with excellence. Journalism's mission, like education's, is too complicated and varied for that to be possible. It must embrace variety in order to inform different audiences, to engage them civically, to both challenge and nourish their ideas, and to offer a forum for opinion. It's a big job.

What all this suggests is that the actual determinants of journalistic excellence — where and when it occurs and in what degrees — are cultural. By "cultural" I mean that it is complicated, diverse, multicausal, and difficult to sort out — but not hopelessly inscrutable. Journalistic excellence is a complex *social* relationship. It does not grow on trees and cannot be done by robots. It requires skilled practitioners (professional or otherwise). How good it is depends on their talent, education, experience, and what they ate for breakfast. It also depends on the qualities of the institutions within which they work (such as resources and independence); the professional culture that surrounds them; and the culture of meanings they share with their audience, enabling lightbulbs to go on, however brightly or frequently, in some people's heads.

In addition, there are the imponderable influences of contemporary culture as a whole on the communication process; the democratic conversation that journalism feeds, the constant hum and buzz of other background conversations, the noise behind the signal, and so on. So when we talk about journalistic excellence, we are mainly isolating facets of a complicated cultural prism of causal determinants. We are talking about complexity.

3. The Three Graces of Journalism

So what *is* good journalism? We can never hope to arrive at a single incontestable definition; moral, political, and intellectual differences inevitably surface. But at least three basic components are integral to excellence, at different levels of the journalistic enterprise. Each is complex, riddled with both internal distinctions and external connections to the other components. Each is embedded in the broader culture. But we can usefully distinguish three forms of excellence: the moral imperative of truth, the intellectual imperative of context, and the institutional/political imperative of independence.

These three rubrics do not provide an exhaustive account of journalistic excellence, or what it means to be a great journalist or news outlet; but they are crucial windows on what we must now admit to be a pretty complicated picture. They are not isolated or arbitrary windows; they are related and complementary, and each contributes to defining journalism's role in a democracy.

Truth

The most obvious precondition of good journalism — or even of mediocre journalism, for that matter — is truth.[2] Getting at the truth, and not something else, is what usefully differentiates journalism from fiction, rumor, gossip, state propaganda, commercial advertising, public relations, political spin, and assorted other abuses of knowledge (as well as opinions, beliefs, graffiti, and blogging). Journalistically, truth is something we should be able to take for granted, but cannot. It is journalism's most important feature.

Truth, at first glance, has two faces: getting it right, and getting it all. Media-literate citizens engage with reported facts based on informed curiosity — not just "is this really true?" but also, "what else is there?" We want the whole truth and nothing but the truth. Truth, as we shall see in the next chapter, can be a complicated business; but it is not entirely unknowable. And since our context here is journalism, and not the mind or the universe, some of the stickier points can be left to philosophers.

Within the journalistic sphere, there is general agreement that truth is not just a useful concept but the keystone value, central to what distinguishes news from other forms of communication. Reflecting the world as we find it is the main point of the journalistic enterprise, and thus a precondition of any notion of excellence. Without it, we are simply swapping stories — or rumors or poems or gossip. All of these things have their place, but we also need news.

Who, what, when, and where: these framing questions form the basic logical architecture of good journalism. They are the essential coordinates of any truthful account of an event or phenomenon, or of any story, even fictional: the key factual elements that cannot be left out of "the whole truth." Along with "why" and "how," they form the canonical "five Ws and an H" of good journalistic practice. These questions still leave plenty of room for subjective interpretation, for example, in selecting the who, what, when, and where, and even more so in choosing how to describe the why and the how. They are the point of departure — not just for journalists, but for media-literate citizens, scholars and teachers, and ordinary individuals trying to make sense out of everyday experience and locate themselves within it.

Good journalism begins by identifying these truths, and proceeds to explain them. Those explanatory elements — the analysis that follows identification — include the "why" and "how," and perhaps also "what next" and "who stands to win or lose." This explanatory dimension of causes and consequences is obviously more complicated and subjective, and hence resistant to rules or formulas. It involves informed, imaginative, at times even speculative accounts of complex phenomena and relationships. Common sense may suggest a particular mode of explanation. But then, common sense is not so easy to explain or formulize either.

In sum, truth is the polestar of excellent journalism, but while necessary it is not sufficient. Even bad or shallow reporting can be truthful. Facts are where we start from; explanations, interpretations, opinions, and arguments are where we proceed to; decisions, judgments, and actions are where we end up. And it is journalism's job to help us get there.

Context

Facts, images, and sound bites convey little in isolation. Sometimes a picture is worth a thousand words; sometimes a hundred words are worth a thousand pictures. Part of the job of a journalist (or a teacher or scientist) is harvesting facts: the "who, when, what, and where." It is about *collecting* the dots. The other part is *connecting* the dots, by delving into the "why" and "how" to explain things more fully, or to provide context. Samuel G. Freedman describes it as "knowledge of how a momentary event fits into the larger flow of politics or culture or history," or the ability to "relate the microcosm to the macrocosm."[3]

Establishing context in journalism is partly a process of reaching back in time to describe and explain recent events as the results of prior events. It is also what historians do, after harvesting the facts. The *New York Times* columnist James Reston famously called journalism "the first rough draft of history." Historians and longer-form journalists can offer fuller explanations and more context, but all good journalists provide it in some degree.

Although working at a different range, and with different rhythms, techniques, and audiences in mind, the journalist's work is in some ways parallel to the historian's — and the study of history is an excellent training ground for journalism. Each seeks to document human events, and aims for depth, proportion, and significance. Each is involved in a causal inquiry as well as a factual one, seeking to impart contextual understanding.

However, every context is not historical. An event or phenomenon may also have a conceptual or thematic context, a moral or evaluative context, a spatial or geographic context, a psychological context, or some other relevant background conditions, in addition to the temporal one. Context in general addresses the last two canonical questions, "how" and "why," and also addresses the "what" on a more general level than mere identification. Facts may identify the "what" of the story — what happened, or the subject of the report — but context also explains the "what" analytically and in other ways that give it further meaning, for example, by dissecting it or comparing it to something else.

"How" and "why" are interrogatives of a more causal nature than "what." They inquire as to the antecedent conditions and temporal sequence that led up to an event. "Why" is perhaps more open-ended than "how"; it is a nonspecific, all-purpose demand for explanation. James W. Carey, in a seminal essay, mentions four aspects of "why": motives, causes, consequences, and significance.[4]

For our purposes, the idea of "context" itself has several distinct contexts or applications. First, "connecting the dots" by answering questions such as "why" and "how" is central to journalism, and to journalistic excellence. Second, history is the temporal context for the news, a background for what happened yesterday, and for the entire journalistic enterprise. The two meld; today's news is tomorrow's history. Third, journalism itself, in addition to having history as a temporal context, has a moral context that gives it authority and responsibility, and that context is democracy.

Independence

The first two forms of excellence that we have identified, truth and context, are organically connected. The third, independence, is modally connected to those two; it is not a third virtue so much as a crucial condition for achieving the first two. (It is not quite a necessary condition, but more about that later on.) Independence is a cultural condition in the literal sense; it is journalistic freedom from influence or control by forces in the wider culture. It is not about the truth of the journalistic voice, or its explanatory power, but about its integrity.

Because the news is a social product, it can never be produced in a vacuum; hence, perfect independence is chimerical. Moreover, most journalism has both an economic purpose (profit, or at least financial survival) as well as a broad political purpose (providing the information necessary for citizenship). The chief threats to journalistic independence are profit and power. Political advocacy is an essential part of the democratic process, and there are many other forms of interest-based or biased journalism, including religious, ethnic, and professional media, which tend to have a defined and acknowledged purpose and a specific niche audience. The more serious threats to journalistic independence are the less visible ones, political and economic.

As with truth and context, the ideal of independence, as insulation from outside influences and competing agendas, is never absolute. It is always relative to some impeding interest, and the aim must be to maximize it. As a human enterprise, the gathering of news cannot be done without any point of view or with spiritual purity. Perfect neutrality is impossible; journalists who care only about their paychecks are hacks. Active moral, even political, engagement is sometimes desirable. But journalism can be considered excellent only to the extent that it is free of concealed biases or competing and corrupting ends. If the quality of information and explanation is compromised by such biases, democratic discourse is compromised.

Another form of excellence, but closely related to the others, is journalism that makes a difference. This kind of excellence, touched upon in the previous chapter, relates to journalism's revelatory function, its watchdog role in a democracy, and its capacity to catalyze change, typically through investigative reporting that reveals things to the public eye that special interests might prefer to keep concealed. It is about the uncovering of scandalous actions or conditions, and leading to change: legislation, prosecution, and changes of policy, personnel, or institutional behavior.

Investigative reporting, when successful, overturns deceptive or faulty understandings based on appearances, by revealing hidden contrary truths. The disparity is registered as a shocking revelation, at variance with received truths or statements by public figures. Although investigative reporting is generally viewed as one journalistic genre, albeit an important one, its actual democratic function is more significant than that would suggest: the identification of failures of the political process or other conditions of public concern that publicity can help to correct. In fact, it is arguably the most important form of journalism.

Vigilance, as a rubric covering investigative journalism and the watchdog function of the press, readily assimilates to the other three rubrics. Vigilance includes digging out important hidden truths and explaining them, and it requires independence. (Strictly speaking, journalistic vigilance is not limited to investigative journalism; it refers to any journalism that either publicizes or otherwise deters misbehavior, keeping officials honest and reporting when they are not.) But while stressing the other three rubrics as broad conceptual markers, we can note that the vigilance of the watchdog or the investigator constitutes a critical domain of journalistic excellence.

4.   Bad News and the Value of Criticism

Understanding journalistic excellence and its democratic context does not require an exhaustive survey of its opposite, journalistic mediocrity. But it might not hurt to briefly acknowledge the flip side of the ideals we are discussing. The most direct and egregious departures from journalistic excellence are full-scale assaults on truth, such as fabrication, plagiarism, or willful misrepresentation of facts, sources, or authorship. Lesser sins include unstated biases (sometimes reflecting a lack of independence), inaccuracy, incompleteness, and shallowness (lack of context). There is enough bad journalism going around. Here, for example, is the assessment of one journalism school dean:

> Network television has dramatically curtailed its coverage of public policy issues and foreign news. Local television has gone further — has basically abandoned its public trust — as it relies on the police scanner and ever-expanding Storm Center teams to scare the hell out of us instead of providing any meaningful civic coverage. Newspapers are more steadfast, but even here the commitment to such bread-and-butter matters as state government continues to erode. And while the Internet may be unparalleled for transmitting ideas and information, it still generates precious little original reporting.[5]

Recent fabrication scandals, such as the Jayson Blair episode at the *New York Times,* have drawn considerable attention as serious breaches of journalistic integrity. Such breaches generally erode public trust in the media (never high in America to begin with), and in the particular institution. But to the extent that these breaches are preventable, the remedies are straightforward (tighten editorial oversight, fire the offender); and while such episodes are never welcome, they do not permanently cripple news organizations that face up to them and repair the damage.[6] Other journalistic shortcomings of a more structural nature (such as the marriage of news and entertainment values) are not so easily addressed. The best antidote to falsification, bias, shallowness, and most other journalistic sins is not the noose but a strong culture of media criticism, and the editorial rigor that it encourages.

Broadly speaking, media criticism comes in two forms. One kind focuses on professional and ethical lapses, such as errors of fact, misleading statements, imbalance, conflicts of interest, subjection to improper influence, etc.[7] The other kind is more overtly political, and typically claims a slant or unstated bias, for example, in story selection, sourcing, selective use of factual evidence, editorializing, etc. Both types of criticism are important, and they are sometimes hard to distinguish in practice.[8] Critics and ombudsmen in the mainstream media tend to focus more on professional lapses or egregious instances of bias. Media scholars, political journalists, and others more removed from the process may have feet in both camps; few interesting scholarly works on the media are devoid of ideological biases or premises.

In any case, robust media criticism of both kinds is desirable on a number of levels, enriching both journalistic practice and democratic discourse in general. Most obviously, it is a vehicle for journalists' accountability to their professional ideals; the critical voice upholds and enforces standards of ethics and excellence. There can be no excellence unless we can talk and argue about it in a dialogue both within and beyond the journalistic community.

As an imperfect construction of the known universe, journalism comprises a vast shadow world of imperfect (and imperfectly communicated) knowledge, rife with possibilities for omission, distortion, and corruption. A critical culture within the media is thus a crucial mechanism of quality control. (Less efficient forms of quality control include audience size, public esteem, accolades, and awards.) Who watches the watchers, or criticizes the critics? Other critics — and the more the better.

Journalism, however, is not just for journalists, any more than laws are for judges, or elections for poll watchers. A critical culture also has direct implications for citizens. And the second function of media criticism is to invite the public into that conversation — because journalism is for and about citizens in the first place.

Media criticism can open up the journalistic process to citizens in several ways. It makes them part of the mechanism of accountability. At the same time, criticism helps people to understand what journalism is about, why it is integral to citizenship, and what standards of excellence the audience — not just journalists' colleagues — have a right to expect. The best criticism also implicitly promotes media literacy, upholding standards of news consumption as well as of production.

Most of all, by taking journalism seriously, media criticism encourages citizens to do the same. We encourage moral seriousness about teaching and education, and a public role in those sectors, for similar reasons. They affirm that what teachers teach, and what journalists say or write, matter to everyone. Bringing ordinary people into the conversation about good and bad journalism is important for citizenship, just as knowledge about nutrition is important for eating. The more we can know about and demystify these processes — and the media are nothing if not mystifying — the better we can make the system work for us.

The point is not to have a nation of citizen-journalists or citizen-critics, each with his or her own blog or podcast, although that may happen. We still need professional journalists, perhaps more than ever. What we need are citizens who are media savvy, respectful of the media's democratic roles as informer, explainer, and watchdog. Such citizens would be aware of potential corruptions, would be able to demand more of journalism and make better use of it, and appreciate when it is done well.

5. Excellence and Ethics

Another important function of media critics (or the same function where truth is concerned) is to patrol the ethical waterfront. Ethical questions are pervasive because journalism reflects all the complications of social life. Reporting involves intensive dealings with people — as subjects, sources, colleagues, audiences — and people can be troublesome. Producing news means describing a society's basic conflicts and, by publicizing them, creating some new ones. Choices, temptations, pitfalls, and dilemmas abound.

We will not probe deeply into that ethical hornet's nest; journalism ethics is a large enough subject in its own right, and one that has not been overlooked.[9] "Every time a disabled journalist is retired to a professorship in a school of journalism," wrote H. L. Mencken, "he seems to be impelled to write a book upon its ethics, full of sour and uraemic stuff." Besides, questions of conduct comprise a set of problems distinct from those of defining and mapping excellence in conceptual and democratic terms. Among other things, professional ethics tends to focus on clear breaches of principles, such as lying or cheating, whereas excellence is more often a matter of degree, of striving toward ideals and avoiding pitfalls that have more to do with competence than with rectitude. As with the rest of life, we have to go out of our way to be bad, but stupidity is effortless.

Another reason to demur on journalistic ethics is that, while ethical journalism is in general a necessary condition of excellence, it is hardly a sufficient condition. A lot of perfectly ethical reporting is mediocre or worse; if laziness or stupidity were crimes, a lot of journalists (and teachers and other public servants) would be in the penalty box. A clear journalistic conscience and the lack of aggrieved parties, important though they are, must be considered minimal conditions of good reporting, not lofty goals.

With the odd exception, ethical breaches, at least insofar as they affect the content of the news or public trust in journalism, must be considered antithetical to excellence. We expect journalists to act properly in their public roles; what they do on their own time is their business. (Likewise, we consider honesty among politicians a necessary condition for supporting them, but not a sufficient condition — unless of course their opponent is under indictment.)

To be sure, what constitutes propriety in the journalistic arena is not an entirely settled matter; the moral dilemmas that journalists face in the line of duty are varied, important, and difficult. For example, journalists seriously debate the use of anonymous sources. The value of truth, on the other hand, is seldom contested, in journalistic or other circles.

As with ethics generally, the more serious breaches of journalistic ethics are not always the most interesting, or even the most problematic. Lies and fabrications need to be exposed, but subtler corruptions and conflicts may be more difficult to discover or remedy. Of course we should tell the truth and treat people fairly, but we also need to pursue excellence by acknowledging and debating other types of conflict and compromise. Here, too, the more media critical voices the better the conversation.

Finally, we might consider the last-minute hints that Polonius planned to offer Laertes, had the latter opted for journalism instead of succumbing to the allures of fencing and French scholarship: Above all else, to thine audience be true, and see thyself as a public servant. Heed thy critics, or at least listen to them. Neither a borrower nor a plagiarist be. Never deceive the public that you serve. Don't make up stories, manipulate sources, abuse colleagues, or conceal your interests and biases — and don't ever be anyone's whore — and you're halfway there.

6.   The Edges of Excellence

A few qualifying points will serve to round out the concept of excellence. First, it bears repeating that the three general rubrics — truth (a property of information), context (a type of information), and independence (a condition under which information is gathered and disseminated) — merely help to organize the idea of excellence in democratic journalism. They do not exhaust or complete it. Different levels and types of truth, of meaning or context, and of vigilance and independence contribute to the concept of excellence, as do other journalistic values.

Great journalism, for example, often demands courage, because it threatens enemies of the public interest. And great journalism may or may not lead directly to actual change, or to repairing or improving democracy. Alternatively, it may be a force for democratic change (and is rarely the opposite) in an authoritarian society. Knowledge, courage, vigilance, and change are vague and interrelated ideas that cannot be schematized or quantified; they are members of the family of values associated with journalism at its best.

Excellence, again, can be encouraged through criticism. Discussion of what is best and worst improves the average. There will always be mediocrity; but over time, we can raise the bar. American journalism has improved with every succeeding generation, with the possible exception of the last. But we must also judge excellence separately for different journalistic forms and venues.

We sometimes associate the best with the long form: magazine articles, essays, film documentaries, and books (the ultimate repositories of wisdom and twaddle alike). These forms of journalism may tend in the long run to have more impact than sound bites, spot-news reporting, or Web postings. But every journalistic time frame requires separate critical evaluation. At every temporal remove from an event, from the perspective of the daily reporter to that of the historian, there is a different trade-off between the advantages of proximity to the event (such as clarity or freshness) and the advantages of distance.

Every journalistic moment has its own needs, limitations, and possibilities, and thus its own standards. (We may think we need up-to-the-minute news, but do we really care who brings us the scoop, or at what precise moment we learn which celebrity of the day is feuding with Donald Trump, or has adopted an African child?) The competitive rush to be first to market with a story does not always correlate with the urgency of the public's need to know, or with quality reporting; while such competition may promote excellence in some ways, it surely inhibits it in others.

Excellence is also relative to human capital: journalists with talent, energy, imagination, and curiosity. There are never enough of these qualities to go around; and their limited supply is one reason to explore the state of journalism education, as we shall do in Chapter 7.[10] Skills and knowledge count. In addition, excellence is relative to financial resources. Journalism is both labor- and capital-intensive, and can be costly. Money may not matter as much in covering the police blotter or the zoning board; but when it comes to reporting on African wars, or investigating the practices and impact of Wal-Mart or the Falun Gong, it can come in handy.

Finally, excellence in journalism, as in education, may need to be understood within the context of a particular audience, defined by particular needs, interests, or levels of sophistication. Education, of course, involves the straightforward division of the learning "audience" according to age or experience; journalism is complicated by a mixture of motives on both the demand and supply sides. But there is no ideal vernacular for conveying the news to all citizens; no perfect level at which the "mainstream" should be pegged. This is a contestable issue on both political and economic turf. Can any news report fail to leave someone bored, frustrated, or resentful?

In addition to all of these relativizing factors, other values, either nested within the rubrics of truth, context, and independence, or somewhere adjacent to them, bear upon judgments of journalistic quality. One such value is clarity of expression, whatever the medium. Simple, clear language is not a strict prerequisite of journalistic excellence, but (like money) it usually helps, and there can never be too much of it. Another value, not incompatible with clarity and concision, but more suited to the long form, is the journalist's ability to deliver the message with style, imagination, curiosity, or passion. Typically, the more deeply one probes a subject, exploring its meaning and context, the further one strays from the narrow confines of the objective report. This can be journalistically hazardous — or brilliant.

7. Perfectibility Revisited: The Prism of Excellence

For all of these reasons, we speak of relative perfectibility, rather than of perfection, in journalism and kindred enterprises; but we can only try to improve upon what we have by imagining something better. Journalism, like education generally, is special in this regard for several related reasons. One is its range of reference, or, put another way, the scope of its mission — to report and to put in perspective what one reputable newspaper calls "all the news that's fit to print." It is a complex human enterprise, with no single preeminent goal or ideal, although as I have suggested, truth is essential for the news to have value, context is essential for it to have meaning, and independence promotes both.

Another reason to stress limited perfectibility is journalism's supportive role as one of the necessary slats (albeit a weak slat) under Liebling's "bed of democracy." The overall quality of the bed is contingent on the quality of that slat; democracies are only as good as their systems of education and information. Without these, perfect constitutions, wise legislators, and fair elections are of little use.

One index of such quality (however difficult to measure) is the general trust that people place in their news media. This idea was captured in a *New York Times* editorial in the wake of the Jayson Blair scandal, which echoes Bernard Poulet's assessment of *Le Monde*:

> The good of any particular institution depends on its people, but this one depends equally on the confidence that readers place in it, a confidence based on the belief that every day, the paper struggles mightily to get things right. Journalism is an imperfect business, the work of reporting, understanding, and writing about the complexity of human affairs. Like all human enterprises, journalism is not perfectible. But it should always be heading in that direction.[11]

In its conclusion, the *Times* editorial refers to the "perpetual goal of the perfect report." If we can never achieve a perfect report, neither can we aim for imperfection. We need standards to aim for, as well as an idea of indefinite perfectibility — no matter how close we come to the ever-receding ideal. We are trapped in an imperfect world, where journalism and democracy are always works in progress. They are always limited by the flaws and frailties of human beings and institutions, and always less than we might imagine them to be. "Shuffling toward excellence," as one journalist has written, "is better than no movement at all."[12]

Journalism at its best inscribes a broad range of information in the public record. In its breadth, it defies simple formulas for judging excellence. What we do have are important guideposts for making critical and comparative judgments about news. Journalistic excellence is neither a single irreducible value nor a random aggregation of practices or principles, but a family of related values for informed citizenship.

A logical and moral thread connects the levels of excellence we have identified. Truth represents integrity in the relationship between journalists and their subject matter, on one hand, and between journalists and their audience on the other. Context relates to integrity in connecting facts to explanations and creating coherent webs of meaning. Independence represents the integrity of a journalist or news organization relative to the social and institutional environment, and is therefore instrumental to the other values.

Thus, no single model can adequately chart the geography of journalistic excellence. The traditional catechism of "who, what, when, where, why, how" provides a sound framework, but not a template for splendid reporting. James W. Carey goes a step further in resolving the "why" and "how" into "motives, causes, consequences, and significance." We have also touched on some dimensions of scarcity: financial resources, human resources, and time.

The landscape of journalistic excellence is neither completely chartable nor an amorphous *terra incognita*. Like teaching, journalism is not an attainable end-state but an endless process — perpetually necessary democratic work. It cannot be legislated or manufactured. To keep that work going and to do it well, we are at the mercy of our imperfect selves and our fellow citizens. To improve journalism, we must continually talk about and criticize it. And, because journalism is about information, and thus about knowledge, power, and democracy, it is seldom a neutral process like balancing a checkbook or taking out the garbage; it is a fundamentally moral and political as well as an intellectual enterprise.

Endnotes

1. Bernard Poulet, quoted in Adam Gopnik, "The End of the World: Crisis at France's Most Venerable Paper," *The New Yorker* (Nov. 15, 2004): p. 71.
2. I am referring to 'truth' here in both the broader philosophical sense, which raises the question of how any news story defines and conveys a piece of social reality, and also in the narrower sense of accuracy: the absence of misstatement of facts.
3. S.G. Freedman, *Letters to a Young Journalist*, pp. 58-59.
4. J.W. Carey, "The Dark Continent of American Journalism," in E. Munson and C. Warren, eds., *James Carey: A Critical Reader*; also in R.K. Manoff and M. Schudson, eds., Reading the News.
5. T. Kunkel, "Journalism Requires Wide Exposure" *Quill* (July 2002): p. 18.
6. The Jayson Blair scandal, for example, did not lead to a precipitous drop in the quality of news at *The New York Times*, or a drop in its circulation or in the paper's stock price. It did show the Times to be fallible, which some may have suspected all along.
7. An example of criticism of this kind is the "Darts & Laurels" section of the *Columbia Journalism Review.*
8. See, for example, B. Goldberg's Bias, and E. Alterman's *What Liberal Media?*
9. See, for example, K. Sanders, *Ethics and Journalism*; or S. Klaidman and T.L. Beauchamp, *The Virtuous Journalist.* Menken quotation: "Learning How to Blush," in *A Gang of Pecksniffs* (New Rochelle, NY: Arlington House, 1975, p. 111); quoted in S. Bates, "Realigning Journalism with Democracy," Pt. 3.
10. In less democratic cultures, excellence is also relative to the legal or political barriers posed by governments or other institutions to freedom of the press.

11. Editorial, *The New York Times* (June 6, 2003): p. A-32. Note that I am using the term 'perfectible' differently, to mean 'improvable,' rather than (as the editorial uses it) to mean "capable of achieving perfection." *The Oxford English Dictionary* defines 'perfectibility' as "a capacity for progress or improvement, esp. in the attainment of moral excellence..."

12. David Pogue (writing about progress in palmtop computers), *The New York Times* (July 3, 2003): p. G-4.

4

Truth is Tricky

The facts are useful and real. ... They are not my
dwelling. ... I enter by them to an area of the dwelling.
　　　　　　— **Walt Whitman, "Song of Myself"**[1]

1.　The Value of Truth

In most societies, and especially in democracies based on
active and informed citizenship, truth is a prized value: it is a
moral virtue, and untruth a sin. Wherever there is an intellectual marketplace — wherever there is human communication
— there is a natural demand for truth, and also a demand
for at least relative certainty, to the extent that certainty can
be obtained. Communication without standards and expectations of truth-telling would be like traffic without roads. Thus,
formal communication, including journalism, generally puts a
high premium on truth.

This penchant for veracity (from, if not toward, others)
may be a cultural trait rather than a biological one. Perhaps
early hominids found it expedient to lie their heads off to one
another. Perhaps, prehistorically, if your neighbors lied to you
about where the woolly mammoths were lurking, you lied right
back to them (if you survived), and mistrust prevailed; or perhaps not. But as complex societies emerged, based on forms of
interdependence beyond the family and the tribe, truth became
handy not only as a tool of survival but also to grow your crops,

sell your wares, conduct trade, navigate the oceans, or marry well (or at least know what you were getting). Civilization itself is based on trust in communication, however often that trust is breached.

Truth-telling is a virtue in part because, as with so many moral matters, there's a strong element of reciprocity; even the most accomplished liars prefer not to be lied to or deceived. Thus, dishonesty is proscribed in most cultures, and the areas where truth-telling standards are relaxed are more or less clearly defined: story-telling, art, entertainment, advertising and public relations, talk radio, and the blogosphere. Mainstream journalism, so called, is not one of them.

Lying is not just hard and dangerous work; it harms and manipulates people, and we do not want to be its victims. Thus we prefer truth to the alternative as we prefer fresh air or food. Certain types of information, such as about government and society in general, are of particular importance to democratic citizens. That, of course, is the knowledge that is journalism's first business to convey.[2] Indeed, truth-telling per se is not enough. Good journalism must also be vigilant in order to expose, wherever possible, lies, evasions, deceptions, omissions, and bullshit.

Lest we get carried away, factual truth, like anything else, can be overrated in some contexts — but journalism is not one of those contexts. Creative fictions are often more interesting; but they involve a different social contract with the audience, including a great deal of fine print (especially when closely based on factual events), as well as a different audience.

More to the point, a strictly accurate but superficial account of an important event is not necessarily or uniformly better, in terms of the overall public good, than one with greater explanatory power that contains some minor inaccuracies or even basic untruths. Even moral principles, if too narrowly construed, can blind one to consequences, and thus lead to collisions with other principles. Literal truth does not always entail balance or fairness (which are not always the same thing). Yet we must and do defend truth in general; journalism that deserves the name promises its audience, as part of its duty to democratic citizenship, not to stray into the realms of deception, omission, or imagination. However many ways there may be of perceiving an event, it is journalism's obligation to perceive it with integrity.

2. Truth Is Pragmatic

Like most big metaphysical decisions, the cultural sanctification of "the truth" as a unified reality underlying our fallible thoughts and words (as in Walter Cronkite's noted sign-off, "That's the way it is") is ultimately a pragmatic one. It ignores, among other things, the obvious fact that we often perceive truth differently and cannot always reconcile those differences, because there is no ultimate arbiter of perception.

For most human discourse, and especially for journalism, it is useful to presuppose such a unity — according to which time is linear, objects are stable (quantum theory be damned), things exist or occur in only one way, and every event has a cause, regardless of our varying descriptions and accounts — than to suppose otherwise. As D. T. Z. Mindich writes, "There is an out there out there."[3] In fact, most human communication and interaction implicitly presume a Newtonian universe, a more or less fixed whole (or at least a whole that is changing in more or less fixed ways) that we can usefully call reality.

Nevertheless, it is unwise to talk about "the way it is" on a grandiose scale as if we could somehow capture the world whole in our speech. "Reality," as Hannah Arendt observed, "is different from, and more than, the totality of facts and events, which, anyhow, is unascertainable."[4] If reality means anything, journalism only scratches the surface of it, and journalists have no more idea than the rest of us about "the way it is." They just know more about certain current events. The problem is not that the past (or present) could occur in more than one way; it is that we cannot possibly see it whole, or see it in exactly the same way.

Relativism and relativity have their place. We can argue ad infinitum about what "truth" means, either in general or in a given situation: what transcends different subjective perceptions, different ways of perceiving, and different values. But meaningful communication requires agreement on at least a handful of indisputable facts, which are part of the fabric that we can usefully call "the truth." Such facts are not just relevant but essential to the coherence of everyday experience and language. Without them we could scarcely do more than bark or grunt. What journalism needs, as Bill Kovach and Tom Rosenstiel note,[5] is a "practical or functional form of truth ... a process — or continuing journey toward understanding ...

> [It] is not truth in the absolute or philosophical sense. It is not the truth of a chemical equation. But journalism can — and must — pursue truth in a sense by which we can operate day to day ... It is actually more helpful, and more realistic, to understand journalistic truth as a process — or continuing journey toward understanding — which begins with the first-day stories and builds over time ... knowledge is a process of accretion, not of simple extraction. Facts and understanding build and change over time; like news stories, they don't simply pop into being, they develop.

Indeed, journalistic truth, as a nexus of much social communication, is perhaps the most pragmatic variety of all. Whatever its other problems, they are not those of philosophical conceptions of truth, which must clear a higher metaphysical bar. To deny the very possibility of such truth is to question democratic life itself, or social life of just about any kind, for that matter. Besides, journalists have no time for such debates; they need to get to the fire, find out how it started, and file a report.

Truth, then, is not a fantasy or an illusion. It is a pragmatic construct and a reflection of our common experience of the world. We distinguish truth in various ways from error, lies, exaggeration, imprecision, inaccuracy, propaganda, or blarney — not because the distinctions are always obvious or natural, but because they are useful intellectual and moral devices. Truth may be a "mere" convention or human artifice. But then, when you take away human artifice there is not much left over for philosophers to pick through. If truth is not inscribed into the very fabric of the universe (and at least some of it is not), it is nevertheless all we have — and all we need.[6]

Where truth cannot be ascertained, we must acknowledge the spheres of opinion, conjecture, uncertainty, confusion, and contestation among conflicting values, while arguing until the cows come home about normative matters such as tax policy or abortion. Those debates are perpetual, at least until there are major shifts of opinion and the formation of consensus (as there is now, for example, a consensus about the virtue of democracy itself or the evil of child labor, slavery, or genocide). Argument alone does not change minds or reshape consensus. But to have those debates in anything but a purely abstract philosophical context, we need at least some facts to agree on.

Not trusting in facticity because facts can get philosophically complicated if we look at them too closely is like not believing in free will because causality is complicated and determinacy of certain kinds has explanatory power as well. Whatever the case for determinism (and it is stronger in the realm of science and nature than in the messier human arena), we have no choice but to believe in free will of some kind; every act assumes as much. Likewise, however complicated facts may be in theory, they are hardly impossible or delusory, and without them we would get nowhere, and journalism would not exist.

3. Truth and Accuracy

There are various levels or types of truth, including levels of journalistic truth.[7] The first and most obvious for journalistic purposes is accuracy, which might be defined as the direct correspondence of a message to a specific antecedent reality that it purports to represent; a quote, to take the easiest example. (Yet even an accurate quote cannot reflect the tone, context, or unspoken thoughts or intentions of the speaker.) Accuracy is journalism's Ground Zero, where everything else begins; it is closely linked to another of truth's hobgoblins, objectivity (more on that later), and to the celebrated first four Ws: who, what, when, where. If you cannot get the names, numbers, and quotations right, why bother with the rest?

Accuracy alone, with respect to pertinent facts, is not a sufficient condition of the overall truth of journalistic narratives; it is merely stenographic. Those narratives require more than stenography, and may be consciously or unconsciously biased or skewed in many other ways: through selection, emphasis, tone, structure, and so forth. Accurate representations may mask egregious omissions or unwise selection judgments. And while inaccuracy is never desirable or excusable, it is not the worst sin (fabrication gets that nod), and some types of inaccuracy are more serious than others.

Inaccuracy, moreover, is among the easiest of journalistic sins to detect and correct. The failure to provide context, relevance, balance, or fairness; lapses of vigilance, lack of independence — these are harder to discern and to remedy. It does not excuse inaccuracy to say that failure to get the story at all (or to report it in sufficient depth) is a greater sin, and harder to correct, than getting a stray fact wrong here or there; but of course, it depends on the fact.

It is in deciding what is "true" as opposed to merely "accurate," and what is relevant to a fuller understanding of the truth, that we establish the context of an event. (Besides the score, what did the game say about the character of the two teams, and their chances for a playoff berth?) Truth becomes more elastic and complicated as we move beyond obvious facts and toward a narrative account that fills in the background — and the foreground — to provide context and explanation. That is where "the facts" acquire (or reveal) their true meaning.

Accuracy is mainly about surfaces, and correspondences between an object and the report of it; it is where our search for truth begins but not where it ends. Appearance is seldom an adequate account of reality, and almost never the whole of it. Artists understand this as well as anyone. "Nothing is less real than realism," wrote Georgia O'Keefe; "Details are confusing. It is only by selection, by elimination, by emphasis, that we get at the real meaning of things." The Hutchins Commission report made a similar point: "The account of an isolated fact, however accurate in itself, may be misleading and, in effect, untrue."[8] Selection, emphasis, and tone are necessary for the construction of meaning, but they can also make putatively objective facts tell subjective tales.

Journalistic excellence, then, requires more than just stenographic accuracy in conveying antecedent messages (such as facts, images, or quotes). Just as democracy involves more than good laws, journalism involves more than just the facts. It relies on a wider culture of truth: a value system and set of shared understandings and conventions about depicting the world "as it is," and not as it isn't. That culture of truth involves not just the cultivation of objective accuracy, but also the subjective effort to avoid bias, imbalance, or mischaracterization, and the policing of the vast and contested terrain where facts, accounts, explanations, interpretations, and opinions fight their guerrilla wars.

4.   Facts and Beyond: The Burden of Selectivity

Journalism, like the law, must aim for the whole truth (or at least all of the facts relevant to a story), and nothing but the truth. But facts do not swim in a void; facts are human constructs, and are meaningful only when connected to each other and to a context. No one would care that Mrs. O'Leary's cow knocked over a lantern, except insofar as it started the Great Chicago Fire. We must collect the dots *and* connect the dots. We do not gather facts blindly to begin with; we gather them according to some organizing principle. Otherwise, they would be no more meaningful than stacks of pebbles on a beach. Facts need context; when they seem to speak for themselves, it is because we already have a context in our minds into which they fit.

Journalistic truth begins with accuracy, but quickly expands beyond (and with) the facts, in pursuit of such vague and imperfectly obtainable goals as context, balance, proportion, and relevance. All of these contribute to informing the public and holding public institutions and individuals accountable to the public at large.

Facts, moreover, can be sticky, complicated things. They are not discrete bits of the universe that fall into our minds fully formed like ripe berries, nor are they arbitrary or capricious inventions. Like language itself, they are tools, made to fit our mental needs in negotiating reality; and they are not made by philosophers. Facts are practical certainties: propositions which, if not absolutely verifiable, are so likely to be true that their denial is impractical and self-defeating. That is why, once facts are collected, we agree on them. They are by definition islands of agreement in a sea of uncertainty. There may be disagreement about what the facts are and what they mean, that is, their relevance in a wider context; but facts are facts.

Some facts have clearer objective standing (it is hard to refute the score of a ball game or the outcome of a congressional vote); but facts, by definition, are at least in principle ascertainable: they can be verified and shared regardless of one's values or prejudices. If they cannot be ascertained and commonly agreed upon, they are not facts but suppositions, opinions, interpretations, or other expressions of value.

Even when facts cannot be ascertained, we often agree in principle on what is and is not known, what can and cannot be known, and what is important to know. It is unlikely, for example, that incontrovertible new facts will emerge to explain the Kennedy Assassination. On the other hand, we knew more about the perpetrators of 9/11 a week later than we did on September 12.

One of the key functions of journalism is to supply us with a regular flow of the facts we need to know in order to make judgments, formulate opinions and arguments, and function as citizens. But they are only the point of departure for the forming of deeper understanding, ideas, interpretations, and for informing values and arguments: that is, for answering the questions of how and why, and what next.

Once the facts are agreed upon, the real work of constructing meaning, interpretation, and argument begins. This is when the news gets interesting, not just in finding the pertinent facts but in laying them out in a pattern that makes sense. The Hutchins Commission report observed that "There is no fact without a context and no factual report which is uncolored by the opinions of the reporter."[9] Echoing that thought, G. C. Woodward writes that facts "do not announce themselves. They must be selected, ordered, and usually given some larger meaning."[10] And that opens the floodgates of subjectivity; as Woodward further remarks,

> The rhetorical skills of most news makers are largely secondary to the near-total control of form and substance that reporting often permits. Journalism is just another form of portraiture. It requires the selective reconstruction of a reality from a broad palette of materials. Doing the work of journalism means putting one's own perspective on even the most straightforward events.[11]

In other words, the educative power of any journalistic narrative lies partly in the author's voice and judgment: in the ability to serve as a sur-

rogate witness to events; to organize facts into a coherent narrative or ana-
lytical statement; or in the sheer evocative power of the subjective voice.
It would be naïve to suppose that such subjectivity cannot be a vehicle
of meaning, of knowledge, of passion, or that these are not often intertwined. Indeed, extremes of objectivity (e.g., in citing statistics or identities or quotations) and subjectivity (such as in first-person accounts of
dramatic events or experiences) are not just equally potent ingredients of
journalism; often they coexist within the same scene or sentence.

Journalism is quintessentially selective, and selectivity means subjectivity. This means choice, even among objective facts, and human subjects, not gods or computers or public plebiscites, make choices. Even
facts may be factitious. The shower you took this morning is an event few
would find newsworthy; yet it is only by a cognitive process of selection
that we decide that your shower does not qualify as a newsworthy event,
compared to, say, the President's public remarks later in the day.

News judgment is a complex and mysterious process of triage that is
left to journalists to perform. Their decisions are often influenced by legal,
commercial, or technological factors as well as by personal factors and
professional and cultural norms. Controversy and conflict are generally
deemed more newsworthy than agreement and peace. Bad news drives out
good news (often for good reason). Drama, emotion, and conflict are more
news friendly, if not more newsworthy, than nuanced analysis of evolving
trends or causal explanations of Big Social Forces.

"An eye for the significant detail" is a journalism school mantra: find
the facts that are most revealing. But which facts are those? And what if
two equally true and seemingly significant details tell different stories, or
different sides of the same story? It can happen. Just how far must a journalist go in unraveling the context and meaning of events? It is a judgment
call. Standards of truth, as Max Frankel points out, are much lower in the
popular media — film and television for example — than in the mainstream news media, where untruths, when detected, are condignly pun-
ished.[12] "Facts, unlike literature, do not promise truth," Frankel writes:

They only record what has been seen and heard somehow, by someone, subject to all the frailties and biases of their observers and

interpreters. Yet they must be defended, particularly in a society that values freedom, because by definition, facts can be challenged, tested, cross-examined. Wrong facts and the truths derived from them are always correctable — with more facts. Fictional facts are forever counterfeit.

5.   The Meaning of 'Objectivity'

In any language or culture, the prize form of knowledge is certain knowledge — that which cannot be doubted or questioned. And so it goes for journalism: when absolute certainty is unobtainable, relative certainty is a value; being pretty sure beats being fairly sure and both beat utter confusion. Hence, the notion of objectivity, while displaced from its lofty perch of a century ago, still plays a role in conveying, understanding, and evaluating knowledge.

However, objective certainty is a harder thing to come by than was once supposed, especially in journalism with all of its temporal, commercial, cultural, and other limitations. "Objectivity is epistemologically impossible," writes Herbert J. Gans, "because the moment journalists ask questions they select from a large number of possible ones."[13] For the most part, we have to settle for the next best things: limited and relative certainty, and the epistemic humility that is integral to all critical thinking.

Within a narrow factual range, perfect objectivity or something close to it is possible. There is no need to argue about the identity of the president, the price of IBM stock at yesterday's close, or the score of a ball game. "Who, what, when, and where" are relatively fixed factual elements essential to understanding any event. Yet even these names, dates, locations, etc., warrant attention only because a preexisting cultural consensus assigns value to them: a consensus that deems stock markets or ball games (for some people) worth knowing about, and decides which facts are important and which are irrelevant. We may then proceed to argue about the significance of different statistics or the accuracy of descriptions. We may argue about whether a pitch was a ball or a strike, but not about what "ball" and "strike" mean in the context of the rules of baseball, or what the umpire called the pitch.

As Gans suggests, virtually everything that passes for news — and not just sporting events — is in the broadest sense normative, based on value judgments of some kind, if only about what counts as news.[14] Even "objective facts" require some degree of trust and shared assumptions for their successful and useful communication; indeed, any use of language requires it. A headline might read "War Declared" or "War Over" and be objectively true, in a useful sense of the term; but then the inevitable choices begin. And one might still ask: short of a sudden, massive commencement or end of hostilities, what counts as a "war," or as its beginning or end? Everything we can express is in some ways a compromise, and could be expressed differently.

Thus, only a few classes of propositions can be considered truly objective. Some of these are propositions whose truth must be commonly accepted as a condition of any further discourse. These include definitions (although definitions themselves may have shadowy boundaries; usage is complex, and language evolves) and specific identities in time and space (such as names of people and places, or locations in space and time).[15] These objective truths are indispensable; but they are also insufficient bases for communicating meaningful knowledge, which requires not just empirical facts but context, descriptive elaboration, historical narrative, analysis, and sometimes evaluation.

Objectivity is thus a narrow but useful matrix of certainty, in a universe that is full of uncertainty, argument, subjectivity, ignorance, and error. It can neither be exalted as the fountain of truth nor dismissed as irrelevant or chimerical. We must value the limited domain of certainty it represents, and fulfill the democratic mission to inform by venturing beyond those confines into more subjective realms. We implicitly credit less-than-objective news accounts all the time.

We also need to recognize an ambiguity between two important senses of "objectivity." One refers to the status of the *message* in terms of its certainty. Objective messages allow no meaningful choices; they can only be delivered in one way, more or less.[16] No two accounts of Abraham Lincoln's assassination are identical, but it is an objective fact that Lincoln was shot at Ford's Theater on the night of April 14, 1865, and died the following morning in a house across the street. To deny such facts, however otherwise described, is to end the possibility of further discourse.

The other, slightly broader sense of objectivity describes the messenger rather than the message per se. In this sense, a journalist is "objective" not if he or she produces a report that neither contains nor requires any epistemic choices (which is impossible in providing a full account of anything), but if the account is free of discernible bias. What counts as a bias is itself a problematic and contestable question.

These two senses of objectivity overlap, and both occasion important arguments. The first equates with certainty, while the second is loosely synonymous with fairness or balance, especially vis-à-vis competing views or interests.[17] In this sense, we refer to individual reporters or observers as "objective" when they have no axe to grind, or at least cannot be seen grinding one. They are never entirely unbiased, unless they are automatons; but their reporting reflects a good-faith attempt to keep the bias out.

Practically speaking, bias is hard to identify or prove, and equally hard to disprove when alleged. It is not the sort of thing that shows up on an x-ray or MRI. It comes out, if at all, through critical discussion. It is one of the things we need media critics for. Most of the battles over objectivity are fought on this political terrain, removed from the narrower realm of objective certainty; and sometimes the alleged bias is not overt but subtle, unconscious, unacknowledged, or otherwise difficult to isolate.[18]

6. Choice and the Ghetto of Objectivity

Is there an objective standard for determining, in any given case, the presence or scope of objectivity? This question contains at least the threat of a paradox of self-reference. But in practice we can look for the presence or absence of choice or judgment. Where there is choice there is subjectivity, even if it is a choice between two objective facts. Everything cannot be reported; but wherever there is no room for choice, where reasonable people would have to agree (as on the score of a ball game, identity of a place or person, or the date of an event or utterance), there is objectivity.

Virtually any journalistic report longer than a sound bite or headline combines objective facts and subjective journalistic or linguistic decisions. Even the selection and emphasis of objective facts is a subjective process. If journalism were strictly limited to objective truth, it would not be journalism as we know it, and could tell no stories.

On the other hand, if reporting were radically subjective, conforming to no reality or purpose beyond the messenger, it would not be journalism but something else. We have a concept of news because certain facts and events are deemed worthy of being made known to democratic citizens; because sufficient and reliable standards of truth are available; above all because, despite the shortcomings of all communication, it helps to suppose that we share a more-or-less commonly perceived reality.

No one can ever know an event in its totality, much less communicate such knowledge; but we do what we can with the certainty, or near certainty, that we have. The dates of the three-day battle of Gettysburg, which armies were involved, and which generals were in command, are indisputable facts; and they are important facts, on which further understanding and discussion are conditioned. Yet the claim that the North won at Gettysburg is not an "objective fact" but a point of general consensus that nevertheless invites qualification and interpretive argument; both armies suffered heavy losses and squandered opportunities, but the cost was clearly greater to the South. Similarly, it would be hard to argue that the Japanese won the Battle of Midway. Nevertheless, these are interpretations of factual patterns; they are not the same as saying that the Red Sox beat the Yankees yesterday, or that Japan was defeated in World War II. Even terms like *victory* and *defeat* do not mean precisely the same thing every time we use them.[19]

Full and efficient communication requires that we express ourselves at different levels of certainty, as circumstances dictate, from the objective fact to the empirical generality or interpretation, to speculation, opinion, or emotion. Truth and clarity require that we acknowledge which level we are on. It is hard to achieve much certainty, objectivity, or neutrality in any enterprise (such as journalism, education, and many art forms) that centrally involves the use of language. Language itself is a vast, complex array of choices, and choice is the quintessence of subjectivity.

Send a thousand competent journalists to cover the same fire on Elm Street, and you will get pretty much the same core of significant facts in each account, but each will be unique. Most will report that a house burned, who lived there, the time and address; most will mention any known causes and effects, including the number of injuries or fatalities, and get a quote from the fire chief. But everything else — words, details, nuance, etc. — will differ. The chief will give different quotes to different reporters. Subtle value differences may even creep, unbidden, into the reports.

Most of these differences, to be sure, will be insignificant. It is the key facts that matter most of all — not what the reporter happens to think of the fire department or the insurance companies. Nevertheless, each account is a unique report of the event. No matter how much information we share, or how successfully we share it, or how we measure such success, we remain multiple subjects, each with our own isolated consciousness. This is a metaphysical truth — or if you prefer, an exceedingly general statement about the nature of experience.

There is no lurking threat of an excess of objectivity. Rather, the danger lies in oversimplifying reality by claiming objectivity where there is none available, or where there is rampant uncertainty. The ultimate source of subjectivity, however, is neither the message itself nor the messenger, but the receivers: the many diverse subjects that make up the audience. There is simply no telling how people will choose to interpret the information that journalists dish out. Even as an abstraction, the media audience is unquantifiable (except in gross terms), complex, and constantly changing. It can never be fully understood, mapped, or delineated by opinion polls or focus groups. We, the people, are the ultimate wild cards.

Journalism, in sum, is not a predominantly objective enterprise. Journalistic objectivity is important and necessary, but is confined to a relatively narrow class of truths, too limited to serve as the sole standard of excellence. Journalism is not mathematics or science, or even so-called social science. Accuracy and truth matter, but so do judgment, background, analysis, explanation and context, and integrity.

Journalism is about telling, reporting, describing, explaining; it is replete with human judgments, biases, frailty, and individuality. The people who produce it are not omniscient, and they are often tired, underpaid, or angry at their spouses or at the universe. The information they provide is always open to question in terms of its completeness, importance, balance, and fairness; that is the nature of the game. Doing journalism well requires imagination, not just technique or knowledge, and in that sense it is a kind of art.

This is not reassuring news for the democratically inclined. Indeed, it returns us to the paradox noted earlier: the need of democracies for journalistic excellence, coupled with their seeming inability to ensure its promulgation. Different ways of providing civic information cannot be compared or evaluated easily or objectively. It is not like running a car wash or a Laundromat: find the best machines, and wait for something to go wrong. With journalism, there is no ideal delivery system — merely the hope that it will be done well. That is why we need counterbalancing institutions within the news media themselves, including robust media criticism and appropriate institutions of journalism education, as well as a demanding audience.

How can one quantify the confidence a particular reporter has in the veracity of a particular source, or how accurately it is reflected in the reporting? How does one evaluate the judgments that determine whether a given story appears on page one, or at the top of a broadcast? Except in rough comparative terms, which may be revealing but are seldom definitive, it is impossible. Media criticism is no more a science than journalism. Although it may strive in good faith for neutrality, it is seldom entirely free of any bias. It is always perfectible and subjective, full of choices and assumptions, never authoritative, but always part of an important conversation. It is the quality of that conversation that matters most.

Between the subjective and objective poles lies the twilight zone in which most journalism is located. Within that zone, many kinds of journalistic and linguistic choices are made, some of which are necessary and acceptable, and others not. The expression of opinion, and advocacy journalism, in their proper place, are basic ingredients of democratic discourse, as is first-person reporting. "Eye-witness accounts," writes John Carey, "have the feel of truth because they are quick, subjective and incomplete, unlike 'objective' or reconstituted history, which is laborious but dead."[20] As he further notes,

> A distinguishing feature of good reportage is that it combats [the] inevitable and planned retreat of language from the real. However good it is, good reportage cannot, of course, get beyond language, because it is language itself. It is an axiom of modern critical theory that there are no accessible 'realities,' only texts that relate to one another intertextually. But even if he believes this, the good reporter must do everything in his power to counteract it, struggling to isolate the singularities that will make his account real for his readers — not just something written, but something seen.[21]

Indeed, a vivid, accurate, and thorough subjective account is often preferable to a dry recitation of facts. The two are not mutually exclusive; "The good reporter," Carey adds, "must cultivate the innocent eye, but he must not be innocent."[22] The drama and confusion of war provide many examples: A. J. Liebling's first-person description of the invasion of Normandy for the *New Yorker,* for instance, or Tillie Pierce Alleman's riveting eyewitness account of the Battle of Gettysburg.[23]

Because we inhabit the moment, subjectivity is always time relative, whereas objectivity tends (with exceptions) to be a more durable good. What is written, broadcast, or podcast in the heat of the moment may have a shorter documentary lifespan, but nonetheless may have journalistic value. What Liebling or Alleman wrote as journalism or personal memoir now has the brilliant patina of eye-witness history.

Great reporting may also combine observation, contextual knowledge, thought, and moral judgment, all of which require more distance from the event than the typical eyewitness account. This kind of reporting — George Orwell's kind — knocks on the various doors of the historian, the sociologist, the psychologist, and the novelist. Venturing further into the realm of the subjective, there is often considerable journalistic value in literature itself, albeit at a further temporal and imaginative remove from actual events. Great literature is inherently journalistic, even when reporting from the heart or the mind.

7. Truth and Complexity

As for truth, it is two-faced — and that is just its face. The more complicated face is the resolve to discover "what is the case," as in Ludwig
Wittgenstein's elliptical remark that "the world is everything that is the
case": to provide as complete and accurate an account as possible of some
event or phenomenon. This is what we normally call "the truth," and it is
the most we can hope for: more complete and more accurate accounts are
better than less complete or less accurate ones. That is why truth is important even when unattainable in the grand sense.

The other face of truth is the opposite of "untruth": the refusal to
invent what is not the case; refusing to invent is not hard, if you put
your mind to it. Refusing to invent is important for all communication in
which invention is not a clear conceit (fiction, poetry, drama, supermarket
tabloids): truth is central to journalism, scholarship, and nonfiction in
general, including the spoken word — teaching, oratory, and conversation. As the novelist John Hersey observed,

> [T]here is one sacred rule of journalism. The writer must not invent
> … [t]he ethics of journalism … must be based on the simple truth
> that every journalist knows the difference between the distortion
> that comes from subtracting observed data and the distortion that
> comes from adding invented data.[24]

The problem of reporting fully and accurately is not that any particular event may have occurred in more than one way. (It certainly
may be perceived or interpreted in more than one way, which is not
the same thing.) An event can happen only in one way, assuming we
agree that it is an event and did happen, unless we believe in multiple
parallel and intertwined universes. (You never know.) The problem is
rather that, beyond a small core of hard facts, our different perceptions and interpretations of those objective facts spiral out in radically
different subjective directions. Columbus undoubtedly came to the
Bahamas aboard the Santa Maria in 1492. From the standpoint of
Latin Europe he discovered the New World, but not from the point of

view of the natives, nor that of the Norsemen who crossed the Atlantic centuries earlier.

Similarly, Americans and members of Al Qaeda would agree that an attack on the World Trade Center took place on September 11, 2001. What divide us are the divergent interpretations, beliefs, and values that radiate from those objective and verifiable facts. Everyone interprets the world in their own way, based on perceptions, beliefs, frames, and values. What journalism at its best can do (like interpersonal communication but on a larger scale) is to provide a common thread of facts so that larger democratic conversations can take place.

Certain facts are undeniable, and we cannot begin our conversations without accepting them; later we can argue about what they mean. Philosophically and scientifically, we may all inhabit separate universes, and all sharing of knowledge may be illusory; but for journalism and for democracy, as well as for everyday life, it's a nonstarter.

A great deal of knowledge about the world *is* very difficult to obtain or to share, or it's knowledge that can be imagined but never be obtained. We can neither measure nor share the sources of our individual consciousness. In the public realm as well, uncertainty abounds. Was there a second gunman on the grassy knoll in Dallas? Where was Osama Bin Laden in 2006? History, journalism, and daily life must constantly navigate between the certain and the unknowable.

In her essay "Truth and Politics," Hannah Arendt wrestles with the question of why factual truth so often seems in conflict with political forces. The broad answer is that facts are legitimated differently than political power. Even in democracies, truth is secondary to the self-interest of governments and elected officials. That is one reason independent journalism is needed as a check against government: to ascertain relevant facts that politicians and governments find it convenient to deny, distort, or conceal. Factual truth, writes Arendt,

> … is always related to other people: it concerns events and circumstances in which many are involved; it is established by witnesses and depends upon testimony; it exists only to the extent that it is spoken about, even if it occurs in the domain of privacy. It is

political by nature. Facts and opinions, though they must be kept apart, are not antagonistic to each other; they belong to the same realm. Facts inform opinions, and opinions, inspired by different interests and passions, can differ widely and still be legitimate as long as they respect factual truth. Freedom of opinion is a farce unless factual information is guaranteed and the facts themselves are not in dispute.[25]

Facts, Arendt adds, do not exist entirely independent of or prior to interpretation and opinion; they must be selected "out of a chaos of sheer happenings" and made to fit into a larger picture. She concludes with an anecdote about the power of common sense:[26]

During the twenties, so a story goes, Clemenceau ... found himself engaged in a friendly talk with a representative of the Weimar Republic on the question of guilt for the outbreak of the First World War. 'What, in your opinion,' Clemenceau was asked, 'will future historians think of this troublesome and controversial issue?' He replied, 'This I don't know. But I know for certain that they will not say Belgium invaded Germany.'

This does not mean that truth is not at times very complex indeed. It is untruthful — and a conversation stopper — to say that World War I began when Belgium invaded Germany; but there is still ample room to argue about what triggered Germany's invasion of Belgium. On the other hand, factual truth is indeed, as Arendt observes, an inflexible tyrant, at least to those who find it unwelcome — including, she implies, most politicians.

Outright lies seldom survive for long where there is diversity of voices and values — even in a highly concentrated and commercial media environment. (When they come from the highest levels of government, they may be referred to in the media as "inconsistencies.") More widespread, and arguably of greater concern, than outright lies are unexamined half-truths, myths, distortions and spin, and the neglect or suppression of controversial stories that are of public interest.

If politics is hostile to truth-telling, Arendt argues, at least there are "ref-
uges of truth" both within and outside of government. "Very unwelcome
truths," she writes, "have emerged from the universities, and very unwelcome judgments have been handed down from the bench time and again
… the chances for truth to prevail in public are, of course, greatly improved
by the mere existence of such places…"[27] Needless to say, the news media,
if sufficiently independent and diligent, are likewise capable of bringing
unwelcome truths to light; and unlike universities or courts, it is their first
responsibility to do just that.

Endnotes

1. *Leaves of Grass*, facsimile 1855 edition, p. 23.
2. There is a subtle difference between how we normally use the term 'truth'
   and the phrase 'the truth'. 'Truth' usually refers to a relation between utter-
   ances (specific or in general) and an antecedent reality, whereas 'the truth'
   refers more directly to that antecedent reality itself — what really exists,
   what really happened, etc.
3. Mindich, *Just the Facts*, p. 143.
4. H. Arendt, "Truth in Politics," p. 261.
5. B. Kovach & T. Rosenstiel, *The Elements of Journalism*, pp. 42-43. NY:
   Three Rivers Press, 2001.
6. One might question such a broad statement and claim that it is similarly
   pragmatically useful to regard "the universe" as having certain "truths"
   inscribed within it. We cannot imagine a universe, for example, in which
   $2+2 = 5$. But ultimately this is a quibble about an unsolvable and arguably
   trivial question.
7. John C. Merrill [*Journalism Ethics*, pp. 113-114] usefully distinguishes five
   levels or forms of truth, which comprise a kind of inverted pyramid. The
   big one at the top, what Merrill calls "Transcendental," or ultimate, truth,
   can never be known or communicated; but it is useful for several reasons.
   It serves to reflect the infinity of possible truths about the world; the relativity and finiteness of the lesser forms of truth; and the entropic nature of
   truth generally. "Potential truth" represents what journalists can obtain;
   "selected truth" represents what they do in fact obtain; "reported truth" is
   what they communicate to their audiences; and finally, "perceived truth"
   is what those audiences, in Merrill's words, "select and ingest from the
   reported truth."

8. R. Leigh, ed. *A Free and Responsible Press*, p. 22.

9. Ibid.

10. Gary C. Woodward, "Narrative Form and the Deceptions of Modern Journalism," in R.E. Denton, ed., *Political Communication Ethics: An Oxymoron?* (Westport, CT and London: Praeger, 2000; p. 132).

11. Woodward, op. cit., p. 133.

12. M. Frankel, "The Facts of Media Life," *The New York Times Magazine*, Sept. 27, 1998, pp. 32-34). "It is unforgivably wrong," Frankel writes, "to give fanciful stories the luster of fact, or to use facts to let fictions parade as truths. The authors of hybrid 'factions' and 'nonfiction novels' claim poetic license to distort and invent so as to serve a 'higher truth' than — sneer — 'mere journalism.' But why then won't they create fictional names and characters and pursue their higher truths in imaginary plots? Why usurp the label of history while rejecting its disciplines? The answer is that fiction and fact live in radically different emotional worlds and the fabricators greedily want the best of both. Fiction thrills by analogy, by the reader's knowledge that unreal plots can illuminate the deepest truths. Nonfiction excites by experience, by extending a reader's knowledge and understanding of reality. Why should not writers, editors, producers and publishers pretend, like carnival barkers, that fictions are facts? Because a reader who is lured into the House of Facts, poor sap, has paid to experience facts."

13. H. Gans, *Democracy and the News*, p. 151 (note 7). John Merrill [*Journalism Ethics*, p. 20] puts it another way: "One must admit that a reporter, trapped in the inadequacy of language and personal psychological and ideological conditioning, cannot perfectly objectify anything in communication."

14. On the normative nature of news, see, e.g., J. C. Alexander, "The Mass News Media in Systemic, Historical, and Comparative Perspective," in E. Katz & T. Scecskö, eds. *Mass Media and Social Change*. Beverly Hills: Sage, 1981.

15. Necessary truths include logical propositions, statements that are true by definition, and mathematical equations; they have little direct use in journalism. Likewise, very general empirical statements that are virtually necessary within human experience (such as that the sun rises in the east each day) are seldom newsworthy; they are more like what Kant called synthetic a priori truths. Objective truths include accurate identities and figures, verbatim quotations, dates, statistics, and measurements (any of which may nevertheless be partly subjective insofar as they are selected from a range of possibilities, including no selection).

16. There are always different ways of stating objective facts, e.g., that it is now 3 p.m., or that the President lives in the White House. Trivial as they may seem, they show that hardly any communication (except on multiple-choice tests) is confined to a single utterance. In the strictest sense, the decision to say or write anything — to communicate in any way — is a choice.

17. Robert M. Entman (*Democracy without Citizens: Media and the Decay of American Politics*, p. 30 ff.) cites two "objectivity rules" relevant to this second sense of objectivity: depersonalization (not giving one's own point of view) and balance (giving two points of view fair treatment). Neither of these worthy aims is absolutely attainable. They are indeed the bases of fairness, but not of objectivity in the strictest sense, which is limited to logical deductions, mathematical truths, or unchallengeable claims such as statements of identity ("The president is a Republican"). Thus, while depersonalization and balance are usually necessary, they are not sufficient to prevent any and all slanting; there are simply too many ways in which coverage betrays subjectivity. Moreover, there are some circumstances in which personalized coverage and a point of view or attitude are acceptable, and where balance does not amount to fairness, e.g., where different arguments (flat-earth advocates, Holocaust deniers, etc.) do not deserve equal attention.

18. For example, is it political bias, selective truth, or insightful analysis (or a combination of the three) to compare Hillary Clinton's oratorical skills unfavorably to those of her husband, Bill Clinton, as *The New York Times* did in a news story about the funeral of Coretta Scott King in February 2006 — and then follow up with another story exploring that unfavorable comparison?

19. For example, it is convenient and meaningful to say that the Allied Powers "won" both world wars. But it is misleading unless one distinguishes the two cases as different ways and degrees of "winning."

20. Carey, "Introduction," *The Faber Book of Reportage*; p. xxix.

21. Carey, op. cit., p. xxxii.

22. Carey, op. cit., p. xxxiii.

23. T. P. Alleman, *At Gettysburg: Or What A Girl Saw and Heard of the Battle.*

24. J. Hersey, "The Legend on the License," *Yale Review* 75:2 (Winter 1986): p. 290.

25. H. Arendt, "Truth and Politics," in *Between Past and Future: Eight Exercises in Political Thought* (NY: Viking, 1961); Penguin Books, p. 238.

26. Arendt, op. cit., p. 239.

27. Ibid., p. 261.

5

News and Knowledge

To traverse the world men must have maps of the world.
Their persistent difficulty is to secure maps on which their
own needs, or someone else's need, has not sketched in the
coast of Bohemia.

— **Walter Lippmann, Public Opinion**

1.   Knowledge and Complexity

Our use of language attests to the fact that there is such a
thing as knowledge; but it is an exceedingly diffuse thing,
and the epitome of complexity.[1] What usefully counts as
"knowledge" is, to say the least, a broad and diverse class of
conscious states, types of stored information, and modes of
understanding; and the totality of knowledge, whether in a
single mind or sloshing around in the universe, is something
altogether unknowable. We can make rough comparisons,
like "X knows more about A than about B," or "X knows
more than Y about C." We can test people to measure certain
types of knowledge with some degree of accuracy. We can
learn and remember things, but knowledge comes and goes
— just ask anyone with dementia.

News is a kind of knowledge; or at least, information
intended for assimilation as knowledge. *Information* normally
refers to what is more certain and specific, and *knowledge* to
what is more general; but the boundaries are vague and porous,

so there is no point belaboring the distinction. In order to fully understand the idea of journalistic excellence, we need to consider what kind of knowledge the news represents, and what its limits are, beginning with a few observations about knowledge in general.

As a point of departure, we may recall the obvious enough point that journalists, like teachers and others, are not omniscient. Just as there are limits on learning generally, there are indefinable limits on people's time, energy, resources, and capacities to produce or consume news, and on what any one person can know and retain. So we are talking about optimizing, not about achieving perfection.

It seems reasonable to suppose that the civic knowledge citizens need from the media includes basic (and especially new) facts and ideas about democratic citizenship itself, government and law, and prevailing political, economic, and cultural conditions. Such civic or "news knowledge" is naturally related to academic disciplines such as history, political science, economics, the natural sciences, etc.; but it differs in its sources, methods, delivery systems, and audience, as well as in its structure and content. Just as the news should not be confused or combined with gossip or rumor, which we can get elsewhere, it should not be confused with scholarship.

Responsible journalism, however, respects scholarly inquiry, and reports on it when of public interest, avoiding the latent hostility to higher learning that is endemic to American culture. The two extremes, anti-intellectualism and academicism (a problem mostly within the academy itself and learned journals), are antidemocratic; the first is inimical to the core mission of democratic journalism, which is to report and explain relevant new facts, issues, and trends to the general public, while the second is inimical to the democratic role of education. The ideal citizen is not a scholar but a civically literate and media-literate person. This dichotomy between the ivory tower and the public square will loom large as we consider the problems of journalism education.

In practice, the information we need for citizenship can never be identical to the information we get from journalism per se. It comes from many sources, including formal schooling, personal experience, popular culture, the commercial and other news media, family, and community. These various sources may be quality-controlled through a culture of criticism. No single source provides the perfect elixir of civic knowledge. Journalism, however, derives its moral authority from attempting to provide such civic knowledge.

Even art resembles journalism, as a mode of communication that may inform and stimulate — and literature most of all. John Dewey wrote that "Artists have always been the real purveyors of news, for it is not the outward happening in itself which is new, but the kindling by it of emotion, perception, and appreciation."[2] (Well, yes and no.) Art, like journalism, is essentially communicative and revelatory, part of a larger public conversation, and is sometimes explicitly social or political. The most obvious difference is art's unlimited access to the imagination, and its lack of commitment to the stenographic reproduction of certain aspects of social reality, to which journalism is committed.

Knowledge assumes many forms and degrees, and must not be confused with intelligence, another complicated phenomenon that describes our relative ability to assimilate, store, process, and apply knowledge of various kinds in order to model and manipulate our environments. Knowledge is a matter of acquired facts, conceptual models and frameworks, skills, and mental habits. Perhaps most of all, it is an evolving, unconscious, amorphous internal gyroscope based on accrued experience, memory, and formal learning, which indicates (very fallibly) where the connections and boundaries of social existence lie.

It is the function of formal education, not journalism, to provide us with most of our fundamental understanding. The simpler job of journalism is to help us understand our immediate times and situate them on those intellectual foundations. So journalism is typically more mundane and factual than the study of, say, history or philosophy. But their respective functions naturally approach and sometimes overlap one another.

Excellence in journalism, as in education, is not just about transmission or reception. The value of the transaction ultimately depends on the skills of communicator and audience alike: among other things, it depends on their motivation, intelligence, prior education, interests, and needs.[3] Knowledge arrives in our minds, stays, and leaves us with little fanfare or formality; it is ephemeral and evanescent, like fairy dust but more useful. We derive knowledge of society (along with misinformation) not just from journalism or text books, but also willy-nilly from live enter-tainment, soap operas, novels, and popular media; from conversations, dreams, friends, family, or passersby. Knowledge is wherever we find it and whatever we deem possible and useful to know.

Some forms of knowledge are more permanent than others; most learn-ing is gradual, and most knowledge evolves in our minds, with varying degrees of certainty, clarity, and completeness. Journalistic knowledge, although crucial as an historical archive and a form of collective memory, is also relatively impermanent and nontransmissible in real time beyond its immediate audience. Newspapers turn into proverbial fish wrapper; broad-casts literally disappear into the ether, or are digitized and stored on the Internet for doctoral candidates in the twenty-fourth century. People are also secondary transmitters of news, as of disease; as citizen journalists we inform one another, with varying degrees of reliability and completeness, when we gossip or blog.

Ultimately, knowledge has unknowable limits. We could all know a bit more than we do, and probably wish we did; but we cannot know everything, or even imagine what knowing everything would feel like. We can have only a vague sense, at best, of what it is that we do not know. And knowing is not our only pressing business. As we consume media or experience the world, we continuously choose unconsciously between knowing A and knowing B, or between knowing and other modes of experience (to the extent we distinguish them), such as work, family, entertainment, recreation, or repose. Knowing can take the place of doing (the dishes, for example), or of working, eating, sleeping, or playing; but it may also derive from or enhance any of those activities. You never know.

2.   Defining the News

Generally speaking, what we call *news* is information (and any attendant analysis or explanation) that is printed, posted, or broadcast regularly, and intended mainly to inform rather than to entertain, scandalize, or beguile. It is the transmission of civic knowledge — including what we need to know to be political, economic, and cultural citizens; some forms of news, such as traffic and weather reports, support all of these functions. But again, the boundaries are imprecise; we learn from playing and take pleasure in learning.

Just as all education is not formal, neither is all journalistic education. We may learn useful truths about public affairs from any source, including while engaging in a criminal conspiracy or visiting the dentist; a local or network newscast may be more or less informative than an episode of *The West Wing* or *The Daily Show*. This does not obviate the need for journalism, however. As with knowledge in general, there are boundary problems inherent in the very concept of news; but they do not make it a flawed concept, just a complicated one.

In one sense at least, all knowledge is subjective: although it may be stored in books, computers, or databases, it is produced by and housed in individual human minds. Yet news, as a form of social knowledge, is also radically *intersubjective*: it is knowledge that is intensively, if imperfectly, shared, after being pre-cognized and then wholesaled to us by journalists. In this as in other ways it is more like education than the homemade knowledge we fashion in our daily lives from observation, casual conversation, subconscious processes, etc.

In short, news is social knowledge not only in its content but in its public origin, design, packaging, and modes of delivery. As such, it shares some features with personal experience (e.g., the individual reporter as correspondent or eyewitness), others with scholarship (the research and explanatory functions and precognition), and still others with the varieties of entertainment that share its media of transmission.

News is mostly about what is new — recent public events or matters of public interest — and relating the new to the old by putting it in context. As one writer explains, "Characteristic of journalism is its claim to present, on a regular basis, reliable, neutral, and current factual information that is important and valuable for the citizens in a democracy."[4] At its simplest, the news aims to provide what the philosopher Harry G. Frankfurt calls "… accurate representations of a common world."[5]

Like all forms of knowledge, news is partial, problematic, and imperfect. Even its definition is necessarily imprecise; precision, after all, has costs as well as benefits. Greater precision would not necessarily obviate arguments about whether this or that is "news" or "journalism"; it would only narrow the range of the term arbitrarily.

We may not agree about the bounds of the "common world," or whether language more often describes or constructs that world, or whether there is an "ultimate" or singular reality. But those arguments do not help us very much as citizens. We still need to know who did what to whom, when and where, and (acknowledging the greater subjectivity of explanation and context) how and why.

Such information may in theory issue from any source: mainstream or alternative journalism; government pamphlets or reports; trade journals; business, church, or school publications; blogs or Web sites; or secondhand from someone at the corner bar or nail salon who just decides to share. All civic knowledge does not come from journalism, and conversely, everything that institutional purveyors of information may choose to disseminate is not worth dignifying as news. (And who decides who is a journalist?) But the bottom line is that we can usefully distinguish news as a form of knowledge from other forms. And it has some distinguishing features.

First, news is primarily new: knowledge of significant recent events; all the rest is context. Our very definition of an "event" (outside of history) is shaped by an implicit notion of what is significant: what affects us, or many of us, as a community or society. Even many abnormal events (with obvious exceptions such as major disasters) are in some sense ordinary: scandals, elections, laws passed or thwarted, crimes committed or solved, natural disasters, riots, and deaths of important persons. Much of the panoply of information that we think of as news is interesting but not shocking; it is old wine in new bottles. It is neither boring nor fascinating.

Second, news is primarily about change, because that is what we mean by an "event" and "new": a rearrangement of human or natural affairs, making yesterday or last week different from what came before. It is primarily about matters concerning the public in general — hence the preeminence of political and economic news (money rules the world, but politics and the law rule money); it is also about things and values that we share as social beings, such as medicine, weather, natural or social disasters, crime, sports, or traffic conditions.

Third, journalism is essentially regular in frequency and format; it is produced for public consumption at expected intervals, daily or otherwise (sometimes nonstop), rendering it (according to the interval) more or less useful for its proximity or distance from events, and having an unstated shelf life.

Fourth, journalism is to a degree colloquial, but subject to conventions and professional values (such as truthfulness). So it tends to be intermediate in tone and explanatory depth — as well as in cost, timeliness, authority, and availability — between gossip or rumor and scholarship.

Fifth, insofar as it shares both delivery technologies and economic bases with political forces and commercial entertainment, news is embattled. Its independence is perennially subject to compromise by non-news values, commercial, ideological, or otherwise. News is not, like money, stored and exchanged in a neutral quantifiable currency. Rather, it is composed of language and images; and language, as we have seen, is very subjective and a frequent carrier of overt or covert values. Images can be value-laden as well, given an inference or two about their selection.

Historically, this complicated and often conflicted social institution is, notwithstanding its democratic burden, mainly the child of economic forces. As Kenneth Minogue observes:

> [J]ournalism emerged from the specific interests of princes, merchants, and administrators. A prince needed to know something of foreign powers, and his ambassadors sent him back reports, just as a merchant needed to know of profitable opportunities and conditions of trade. A universal institution such as the Papacy needed a constant flow of information. The Greeks, Romans, Chinese, etc., were great annalists, and Herodotus is credited, as the father of History, with creating prose literature out of an assemblage of contingencies, but the drive of most of these writers was precisely to get beyond contingency and find a broader explanatory structure.[6]

With the rise of the capitalist merchant class (and the concomitant, if lagging, expansion of democratic rights and citizenship) came the need to have things reported and explained: mostly business things, but gradually political and cultural ones as well, not to mention science and technology. Thus, modern society is partly defined by the emergence of certain characteristic social institutions and related modes of personhood: the democratic citizen, the believer, the bureaucrat, the merchant, the professional; the worker, consumer, teacher, farmer, scientist, association member. Each of these roles places us in a complicated social web, creating inducements or imperatives for certain types of timely, vernacular, and relatively unbiased social knowledge.

Time imposes costs and benefits on knowledge in intricate trade-offs. (Time lost cannot be regained; "Experience," said Shakespeare, "be a jewel ... purchased at an infinite rate."[7]) We roll toward the future, always at the same inexorable pace, trapped, as it were, in time's barrel. At any given moment, we need facts, context, and critical judgment about the passing stream of events. And our knowledge rolls as well, becoming fuller and deeper but less immediate, relative to particular events, as time passes. News is the "first rough draft of history," in James Reston's phrase; and we always need both first and later drafts.

In fact, journalism at its best complements history in two ways. It explains events in the present by showing their connections to historical events; news is the result, history the cause. We create knowledge by seating facts in historical as well as in other contexts. And, as journalistic accounts recede over time, they become part of history itself, and an archive for future historians. There is no precise temporal or logical boundary where one stops and the other begins.

3.   Narrative and Explanation

Several basic forms of discourse, common to almost all use of language, are involved in the dissemination of news, and they are often tightly interwoven. One is narrative storytelling, which is essentially episodic and dramatic, and framed by time, human conflict, and coherent successions of discrete events. Thus one basic form of news story leads with the announcement of an event, then recounts preceding events in sequence, citing causal connections, and typically includes comments about those events from participants, experts, interested parties, or disinterested bystanders. The basic factual coordinates of "who, what, when, and where," are de rigueur.

The explanatory/contextual dimension of "how" and "why" occasions a second form of discourse, in which journalism creates explanatory webs that not only connect the recent past with the more distant past and with the near future, but also identify things descriptively and thematically. Analysis thus complements episodic narrative; analysis breaks things down (without breaking them); it identifies, dissects, compares, and classifies. Whereas the episodic prism is based on causes and effects, the analytic prism is based on connections and distinctions. Most communication tends to be a hybrid of these two modes. Just as there is an episodic dimension to all journalism, there is an analytic dimension to all language.

Journalists cannot be philosophers. "Processing news," as G. Tuchman remarks, "leaves no time for reflexive epistemological examination."[8] But processing is not the same as understanding, and it is important to recognize the analytic dimension of journalism. It is not just that things need explaining, which is obvious enough. We need to understand events in terms of motives and causes, goals and consequences. Analysis is also about making conceptual distinctions and connections, and knowing when to do which.

The gist of it is this: whenever we make connections we obscure distinctions, and whenever we make distinctions we obscure connections. Most things we talk about have both internal distinctions and external connections that qualify their individuality. It is the explainer's job to make these important distinctions and connections, but also to show which ones they reciprocally obscure; otherwise the world becomes brittle and black and white. This is what Antonio Gramsci meant when he wrote about journalism in his *Notebooks*[9]:

Finding the real identity beneath the apparent contradiction and differentiation, and finding the substantial diversity beneath the apparent identity, is the most delicate, misunderstood, and yet essential endowment of the critic of ideas and the historian...

Making such analytic distinctions and connections is not an arcane philosophical exercise; it is what we tacitly do whenever we speak or write, and a basic cognitive function. Journalists, like teachers, have a special obligation to do so clearly and carefully. Neither recitation of facts nor dry reasoning or analysis can survive very long in isolation; they beg to complement one another. We want to know who, what, when, and where; but we also want to know why and how.

In the meantime, we back into the future, able to see clearly only some of the immediate past and little of the future. Journalists guide us (walking backwards themselves, as guides do), telling us where we are, how we got there, and what may come. Historians lag further behind, sifting the evidence for larger explanatory patterns to provide the widest possible context for the present. For that is what history is: the ultimate context for the present, and for journalism, defined by Edward Gibbon as "little more than the register of the crimes, follies, and misfortunes of mankind."

4.   Foreground, Background, and Context Revisited

The news is mainly about events, and no one can ever know an event in its totality — if indeed it has a totality that is other than hypothetical.[10] Historians may know more, with the luxuries of time and distance, but even they do not know everything that is potentially knowable — not by a long shot. And even what is potentially knowable is a fraction of the "crimes, follies, and misfortunes of mankind" that have occurred. As noted earlier (and as historians would be the first to point out), a subjective eyewitness account of an important event can be uniquely informative. As important as contextual background is, and with all of the advantages of distance and detachment, there is no substitute for foreground. That is where a lot of great journalism begins: with the eyewitness account.

Excellence can be found at either end of this spectrum, or at any point in between. Journalism at its best ranges up and down the ladder of generality, providing both an overview (key facts), the context, and the taste and feel of actual experience to human witnesses and participants. An extreme (but common enough) example of the latter is the soldier's-eye view in wartime, because it is so radically removed from the perspective of

noncombatants. David Remnick recounts in the *New Yorker* how, in reading A. J. Liebling's dispatches from Europe during World War II,

> [Y]ou don't get a coherent idea of the course of the war. There
> is little talk of high politics or the over-all battlefield. But such
> coherence, the editors must have calculated, was the business of
> the *Times* in the short run and the historians in the long. What
> Liebling in his frequent dispatches provided was a richly textured
> sense of the day-to-day reality of occupation, invasion, and battle
> — a foxhole successor of [George Orwell's] *Homage to Catalonia,* a
> forerunner of [Michael Herr's] *Dispatches.*[11]

Liebling was embedded, to use the Pentagon's parlance for its management of journalists during the Iraq War; but he understood and did not
conceal the limitations of that kind of journalism. The soldier's viewpoint
is important, and embedding provides dramatic coverage; more than that,
democratic citizens have a right, if not a duty, to be informed about fel-
low-citizens who are in harm's way.

But seeing a war up close is not the same thing as knowing what is
really going on or what strategic decisions are being made. Embedded
reporters share with the soldiers with whom they are linked a very limited
view of events; and they are compromised by their dependence on those
soldiers for protection. It is a view from which it is almost impossible to
provide much perspective or context. Or as Morley Safer has commented,
"Nobody knows a goddamn thing about what is actually happening."[11]
Only a more detached standpoint can provide the history, strategy, and
policy issues that frame the conflict. Which brings us back to the wider
question of context.

Facts are not the ultimate constituents of knowledge, or even of journalistic knowledge. They are just the smallest observable parts, and the
ones with which we begin. Having too many available facts can be as
confusing and useless as having too few. It is what we *do* with facts
that matters: how we fit them into coherent frameworks of understanding — of social systems, patterns, relationships, causes and effects, and
moral and political questions. Knowledge, insofar as we can generalize

at all, is chiefly about such relationships: about lines and planes and shapes, not just about points; about connecting the dots, not just about collecting the dots.

We tend to form such connections whenever we think: seeing relationships, making comparisons, looking for patterns, making inferences, drawing conclusions. What great journalists (and historians) can do is to point out some of those lines for us. They are dot-connectors par excellence, not just "content providers" but context providers.

That hardly diminishes the importance of getting the facts right, and getting the right facts. Reporting all relevant and reportable facts, or a reasonable collection of them — and not making them up — is the first virtue of journalism, and the easy part. When the shooting stops at the O.K. Corral, the first thing to do is to note the time and place. Next, you count the bodies, find out who is wounded, and who is walking around with a warm gun. Then you try to explain how the ruckus started, and why some died and others survived. Never mind what "O.K." stands for or where Doc Holliday studied medicine. Just get the facts, some choice quotes, and some context — how and why the incident occurred — and get down to the telegraph office. It isn't brain surgery. However, merely reporting that some shots were fired in Tombstone isn't journalism.

Context is not just elaboration of the facts; it is the framework for their very coherence. Samuel G. Freedman calls it "knowledge of how momentary events fit into the larger flow of politics or culture or history ... relat[ing] the microcosm to the macrocosm."[13] Without that background, there is little meaning in the foreground (unless we unconsciously supply the context ourselves, which is often the case). Indeed, most useful knowledge is in some way contextual, crossing or connecting different levels of generality, linking foreground, middle ground, and background, what happened first and what happened next.

Reporting that Jayson Blair falsified stories in the *New York Times* is not terribly complicated. But explaining *why* he did so, *how* he got away with it, and *what it means* for American journalism and American society, requires examination of personal motives, institutional practices, and a host of other questions. The context of the story includes its causes and consequences, its racial and political overtones, its implications for news organizations' hiring and editorial practices, and for the credibility of journalists in general; it also raises questions about how news media cover themselves in a crisis, and how they are perceived and judged by their audience and peers.

Was this an isolated incident, or a chronic pitfall of even the best news organizations, or part of a darker pattern? Did the *Times* lose prestige or credibility, or readers? Did its advertising revenue decline or its stock price fall? How unusual is the event as a departure from normal? What is the immediate and long-term fallout: what comes next, and what will change? Who should be held responsible? These are the contextual questions, which look for the reality beneath the surface. Such reality tends to be different from and more complicated than appearance.

The notion of context is broad by definition; nearly everything we think about either has a context or is one. Everything is related to something else, and we understand things by relating them to what they are not — especially by locating them next to their logical, spatial, temporal, or thematic neighbors. Boats float on water, and day follows night. Context anchors and locates things within the wider universe in which they exist or evolve, emerge or decay. Context surrounds, dissects, relates, and explains, as it keeps the fabric of meaning from unraveling.

In sum, context is the "why" and "how" (and the deeper sense of "what") behind the factual foundations (who, what, when, where). The context of "A" is whatever meaningfully relates A to non-A (or almost-A), including what is located near or next to A; what resembles but is distinct from A; what preceded or follows A; any larger whole that A is part of; and so forth.

The search for context is never an unbounded process, however. There are limits of time, space, resources, and public attention and sophistication. Certain types of stories do not require much contextual elaboration, and some facts, more than others, speak for themselves — which is to say, we unconsciously supply the context ourselves. A news story about an arsonist arrested for starting a fire does not require a history of arson or criminal insanity. Often it suffices to explain, with a few facts, figures, or quotes, how an event came about (not so easy, to be sure, if the event in question is, say, the Cold War or the AIDS epidemic), or in the case of a more localized event, how abnormal it is. Reporting a few facts is one thing; putting an event in context usually means rubbing up against history and wider modes of explanation.

The fidelity of the news to specific events, personalities, and points in time and space is an atomizing force, a kind of positivism, which must be balanced against the holistic, integrating force of critical and contextual thinking. In the end, we do not all have the time or interest to be media critics, much less media theorists. We have only so much time for explanation. We want the news, not an encyclopedia. But news always conveys or implicates other kinds and levels of knowledge.

5.   Critical Media Thinking

Two kinds of knowledge are clearly useful to the journalist in providing context, and they correspond to the two modes of analysis mentioned earlier, causal and conceptual. One is general knowledge of the subject matter, or of the field in which that subject is located (politics, nutrition, hang gliding). The other is specific historical knowledge (including very recent history) relevant to the given event or story.

Journalistic excellence, however, calls for more than just relevant knowledge of the nature and provenance of things or events, or finding the right balance between fact and context. It also requires critical skills for accessing and using such knowledge: the ability to find it, organize it, and analyze and explain it clearly without oversimplifying. These skills are part of the informal logic of journalism — what we might call critical media thinking. They have a counterpart in the similar but distinct set of skills needed by citizens to be critical (media literate) news consumers.

Critical media thinking begins with framing the story, and asking the right questions; not just who, what, when, and where, but how, why, who stands to benefit or be affected, and what next. More than just an interrogatory catechism, it involves imagination, curiosity, mental agility, skepticism without cynicism, and the ability to discover hidden truths: covert causes and effects, motives, victims, interests, agendas, etc. It means renegotiating the boundary between appearance and reality and mapping it for the public. Captain Ahab shouts from the quarterdeck: "all visible objects, man, are but as pasteboard masks."[14] Curiosity, imagination, and the ability to see beyond the world's masks cannot necessarily be taught in journalism school. But a number of critical skills or capacities can be further specified.

First, the critical media thinker has a clear sense of journalism's purpose within the wider democratic ecosystem. That is what makes journalists public servants and not just salespersons or storytellers. Journalism is about democracy; there are things that citizens must know, and are entitled to know, in order for a democracy to function, and there are powerful elites, both within and beyond government, that do not want them known. It is up to journalists to find those things and publicize them. The inevitable lumpiness of democratic government allows people, groups, and institutions to harbor secrets and wield power counterproductive to the public interest. It is up to journalists to compensate by spreading the word.

Second, the critical media thinker has an appetite for complexity, as well as a sense of its limits: the ability to describe complex realities, to simplify when necessary with a minimum of distortion, and never to unduly complicate; there is enough complexity out there already. At the same time, there must be a compulsion for clarity.[15]

Part of such complexity management is the avoidance of binary thinking, of seeing the world as black and white. It is the ability to qualify without negating, to describe shades of gray. Closely related to that is the analytic ability to distinguish and to connect (à la Gramsci), without losing sight of the connections that distinctions obscure, and vice versa.[16] This means seeing the internal variety within things (dissection and distinction) as well as how they are externally related to other things (analysis and connection), while remaining stable entities.

We begin to understand things by individuating them as objects (or objects of thought): seeing them as unified wholes, distinct from their surroundings. Critical understanding begins when we see both their internal distinctions and external connections, recognizing that boundaries and bridges are not, and need not be, clear and immutable; that the world can be both integrated and atomized.

Finally, critical media thinkers must not exceed their authority. When appropriate, they must reveal their own ignorance, or the limits of knowledge in general pertaining to a given subject. This goes beyond the imperatives for truth and accuracy and not plagiarizing or making up stuff; it is about mapping the boundaries of the known, the probable and the possible, the unknown, and the unknowable.

And what about the journalist's counterpart, the media-literate citizen? It is not enough to say the obvious — that journalists must themselves be media literate; nor can we give an adequate account of media literacy here as a function of citizenship, since our main focus is on production and not consumption. But it warrants a passing glance. Here, then, are a few of the basic things media-literate citizens should know:

- How news is selected and reported, and how it might be selected and reported differently.
- Preferably through firsthand experience as students, how to produce, consume, and criticize news media.
- The distinction between news values and entertainment values, and between the civic function of news and the profit motive.
- The difference between criticizing particular media performance and criticizing the media as a whole. How contempt for the news media, by either public figures or citizens, weakens democracy.
- The differences between news, analysis or explanation, and commentary; and the differences between neutral (or putatively neutral) news and advocacy.
- How different media cover the news differently, their respective strengths and weaknesses, and the effects of those different lenses.
- How choices about sourcing, framing, etc., affect the way the news is constructed.
- The differences between news, public relations, advertising, and propaganda; and how various threats (political, economic, and cultural) to journalistic independence potentially limit or slant the news.
- The value of media criticism, and the various ways of critiquing media performance in terms of truth, ethics, independence, bias, etc.

- The compatibility of freedom of the press with the right to criticize, and the difference between criticism and censorship; the right of people — including journalists — to be stupid, wrong, annoying, or unpopular — but not dishonest.

6.   The Problem of Importance and the Cultural Context of News

Joseph Conrad states in his "Manifesto," the preface to *The Nigger of the Narcissus*, "There is not a place of splendour or a dark corner of the earth that does not deserve, if only a passing glance of wonder and pity." It is a worthy credo for journalists. Curiosity and compassion — and an obsession with getting the truth — are all it takes to get started. But since the news is finite in every way (space and time, knowledge and certainty, talent and resources), journalists must make choices and set priorities. Such news judgments warrant the scrutiny of media critics; no surprise there either. Everything cannot be attended to or noticed; attention to news, like news itself, is a scarce resource.

How news values are formed and applied in different institutions are thus matters of general public as well as intellectual interest. Journalism is quintessentially selective, choosing what it deems most important for citizens to know about the recent past; so is all art and expression. And importance is often, but not always, debatable. It is not really debatable that recent events in Iraq are more important to Americans than recent events in Iceland or Bahrain. Just as we cannot report or be informed about everything, we cannot debate everything either.

News judgments are fallible and not made according to mathematical formulas; different conceptions of newsworthiness conflict. We need media critics to sponsor those debates, however irresolvable: to open them up to the public, as befits journalistic issues in a democracy. Questions of newsworthiness and news priorities are part of the cultural context of news. That is not to say they are inscrutable, or impervious to criticism — far from it. In the broadest sense they are determined by the news culture, and the wider culture within which it floats.

To say that the media generally, and news in particular, are cultural phenomena, is a shorthand way of saying that they are connected to, and affect and are affected by, pretty much everything else. Because all culture is inherently communicative, the media's role in shaping and defining a culture is enormous. Media shape the wider culture, and that culture in turn shapes the media. Indeed, the distinction between media and culture becomes even more tenuous when "media" is understood to include mass entertainment and not just "serious" journalism. (Here, too, the critical trick is to maintain distinctions and connections without objectifying either one at the expense of the other.)

Cultures and subcultures are shared systems of identity and communication that connect people to one another along particular lines, divide them from others, and orient them to the rest of the world. Cultures label and locate us, as nations, tribes, and sects, and as linguistic, ethnic, religious, political, or professional groups. As shared ideas, values, meanings, conventions, and customs, they bind us to narrow and broad communities. They entertain and inform and assuage us. The news is part of that matrix of shared information.

Cultures are complex entities — internally diverse and also integral to other phenomena. They may compete, jostle or collide, blur or merge, and can seldom be quantified with precision. They may include stronger or weaker adherents, partial members, unconscious or inactive members, false members, unwilling members, former and potential members. News subcultures, defined by patterns of news supply and consumption, are no exception.

American news cultures (production cultures of journalists and executives, and consumption cultures of audiences) are broad and weak. The audience cultures embrace virtually all literate and even some illiterate citizens, anyone who is exposed to the news media in one way or another. Their internal connective norms are limited (few people, for example, strongly identify with their chosen venues of news, or think of themselves as members of specific audiences). Yet there is considerable congruence between, say, a small weekly newspaper in Florida and one in Idaho, or between TV news stations in midsize markets in Texas and Michigan.

This is partly due to common functions and traditions, and to the general mobility of American culture as a whole.

The overall media culture, in its amorphous breadth, is the most elusive, but in some ways the most important, target for media critics. Cultural issues pertaining to news as a form of knowledge production include: Which cultures are being served, and which ought to be? Which cultures should be recognized, targeted, or catered to? What cultural norms or assumptions on the production side serve, or disserve, the public? How, if at all, can cultures be transcended? When do they obstruct communication or democracy?

7. Journalism and Education

If news and journalistic excellence are core democratic values, so are the production of knowledge and excellence in education. News consumption is only the trailing edge of a learning process that normally begins with formal schooling (and even before that, with informal socialization in the family and community) that contributes, for better or worse, to citizenship. In both the similarities and differences between formal education and journalism, we may further delineate what we are calling news knowledge.

Education and journalism are in the widest sense complementary (if not continuous) foundations of informed democratic culture; both are like vast countries with contested borders — including the border they share. But the correlation between either one and citizenship is imperfect. An illiterate person who is curious, energetic, and informed (through electronic media or hearsay) may be a far more effective citizen than a cynical, apathetic, or bigoted bearer of advanced degrees. And a news junkie who does not vote, speak out, volunteer, or otherwise engage civically is not much of a citizen either. Knowledge is only part of the democratic recipe, albeit an important part.

That said, there are significant points of prima facie congruence between journalism and formal education. Both are deeply rooted social institutions involved in the transmission of knowledge or information from the few to the many. Both comprise vast, roughly contiguous knowledge sectors designed to reflect or interpret the world to us. Much of that knowledge, in both sectors, is highly structured and governed by long-standing conventions; but it may also assume more informal forms such as blogs, group discussion, or conversation.

Education sometimes draws on journalism and vice versa; the two sectors can play well together, at least outside their home institutions. Both shape, and are shaped by, broader cultural forces such as politics, economics, religion, ethnicity, and gender. And what we learn from these two distinct reservoirs (not unlike what we eat) tends to flow not into neatly compartmentalized spheres of knowledge but into a single loosely organized mental soup. We cannot always remember whether a fact or idea came from seventh grade, Shakespeare, or *Charlie Rose*.

Most importantly, formal education and journalism share three fundamental rationales: to equip people for legal and political citizenship, cultural citizenship, and economic citizenship. In both cases, the knowledge producer (journalist/teacher) is the first arbiter of what is important to know, how it is structured, and just about everything else. And in both cases, as in all communicative acts, the relative success of the transmission depends on the skills and capacities of both sender and receiver.

One area of dissimilarity between the two sectors is in the particular skills involved in teaching and reporting. Both involve learning, organizing, telling, and explaining, and may range across a spectrum of audience sophistication; in both there is an element of performance. But the differing subjects, time frames of delivery, and rhythms of the newsroom and the classroom dictate different, if perhaps not incompatible, skills.

Again, journalism is pegged to immediate events of general public interest, whereas education is a long-term, foundational process of building conceptual frameworks and skills. The consumption of news is an informal and voluntary quotidian act, whereas education is more formal and contractual. Education is highly contextual and conceptual; journalism, context notwithstanding, begins with a natural positivism: it is wedded first of all to the spot, the moment, and the fact, and builds from there. Its predominant mode is narrative — storytelling — which is only one of education's narratives. Journalism, more than education, requires storytellers.

Another key difference is that the active, effective transmission of constructed knowledge — which is ephemeral even in a classroom — is not always present or intended when journalism is produced or consumed. Although recounting current events is an essentially educative enterprise, the journalist is not, strictly speaking, a teacher. Reporters mainly want to *interest* (and perhaps engage) their audience, who in turn want to be interested — entertained, enlightened, or both at once.

What is interesting, of course, varies from person to person, and straddles the question of whether the journalist is mainly motivated by civic duty or profit, and whether the news consumer is motivated by the hunger for information, general enlightenment, or entertainment. But more than the traditional classroom, the loose, invisible classroom of journalism is likely to entertain as well as inform, in order to please and retain a paying audience. That, of course, is one of the basic differences between the newsroom and the ivory tower.

Finally, education is a predominantly public (and private nonprofit) enterprise, whereas journalism is mainly commercial and pay-as-you-go; and because of its commercial context, it often blends in entertainment values or substitutes them for news values. As targets of advertising, we ultimately pay at the supermarket and the drugstore to watch Katie Couric deliver the news; but we also pay (civically and intellectually) in our exposure to sound bites and commercially driven information. Universities, on the other hand, are beholden to directors but not to stockholders, sponsors, or advertisers. Independence and resistance to commercial corruption are thus different and narrower issues for education.

8. Excellence and Complexity

A leitmotif of our exploration of journalistic excellence has been the specter haunting many questions about media, communication, and democracy: the specter of complexity. In journalism, as in communication generally, complexity equates with contextual depth, nonbinary thinking, and more layered and nuanced relationships between foreground and background, events and causes, "A" and "non-A," certainty and ambiguity, appearance and reality.

Context in fact represents an important form of complexity. We identify and express things in their simplest form as isolated wholes, internally homogenous and externally unique, apart from their environment. For example, we identify people by their names. What is more complex has more moving parts — that is, more internal distinctions and external connections: for example, a person's life history, relationships, or personality.

Depending on the subject, the journalist, and the audience, complexity may either advance or impede understanding, and so may simplicity; their respective virtues and drawbacks are inversely correlative. Journalistic excellence does not depend on complexity, but on wise decisions about complexity. Time is a factor as well: deadlines, headlines, and sound bites are powerful sponsors of simplification, as is the image compared to the spoken or written word. Longer-form journalism allows more time both for collecting and connecting; in effect, it enables journalists to be more like historians. Thus, magazine articles, books, and documentaries tolerate complexity more than daily news.

Other things being equal, good journalism should convey rather than ignore complexity and ambiguity. But as in all things, there are trade-offs, commercial and otherwise. Complexity has costs in terms of audience size and comprehension; people have limited and divergent appetites for it. Not just journalism but all language and communication are about economies of meaning and complexity; our ideological arguments are largely about competing levels of complexity in our ideas and values.

To communicate is essentially to simplify; complexity is a property of the subject, not a value added to the message; and daily journalism abounds with imperatives, both cultural and structural (economic or technological) to keep it (or make it) simple. Great journalism simplifies complicated stories just enough to make them accessible and clear, without undue distortion. But like everything else, the legitimate demands for simplicity and complexity can never be satisfied by a single journalistic venue, medium, or distance from the event. No formula fits all cases, or all audiences.

Just as the striving for certainty must be tempered by the recognition of uncertainty, probability, and ambiguity, the striving for cognitive simplicity must be balanced by recognition of more complex realities. Messy things must not be explained too neatly; the limits and strength of our knowledge form the most important context of all.

Just as academic writing naturally tends toward the complex — and too often, the abstruse or obscure — journalism, and especially electronic journalism, tends toward simplicity for the reasons described, and too often toward simplification. Both extremes fail their audiences. The profusion of reported or reportable information, culled from the wider universe of observable human and natural events, is limited by the exigencies of both supply and demand, of criteria of significance and relevance, time and talent. It is not a mechanical process like the construction of automobiles on an assembly line, where every rivet has its place in accordance with a blueprint, and every phase of production its precise moment. Rather, journalism is pervaded by the idiosyncrasies, inconsistencies, errors, corruptions, confusions, omissions, and ambiguities that plague any creative human enterprise dependent on skill, ingenuity, and a moral compass.

Endnotes

1. I am defining "complexity" here as the (relative) degree to which something admits useful internal distinctions, and external connections to other things, while retaining its identity. It can be seen that at some point greater complexity has diminishing returns in the economy. What is too simple fails to fully articulate reality as we perceive or conceive it, whereas what is too complex likewise inhibits communication due to obscurity or triviality. Hence, linguistic and philosophical decisions about the use of words and sentences are pragmatic decisions within that economy.

2. Dewey, *The Public and its Problems* (NY: Henry Holt and Company, 1929), p. 184. As Samuel G. Freedman notes in *Letters to a Young Journalist* (p. 26), one-person theater pieces such as David Hare's "Via Dolorosa" or Anna Deveare Smith's "Twilight: Los Angeles, 1992" are also powerful forms of journalism.

3. This is not to say that journalistic excellence is correlative with the intelligence, education, or skills of the receptor.

4. M. Ekström, "Epistemologies of TV Journalism: A Theoretical Framework," *Critical Studies in Mass Communication* 3:3 (2002), p. 274.

5. Frankfurt, On Bullshit, p. 65.

6. K. Minogue, "Journalism: Power Without Responsibility," *The New Criterion* (Feb. 2005): p. 5.

7. *The Merry Wives of Windsor*, Act II Scene ii.

8. Tuchman, "Objectivity as Strategic Ritual: An Examination of Newsmen's Notions of Objectivity," *American Journal of Sociology* 77:4 (Jan. 1972): p. 662.

9. A. Gramsci, *Antonio Gramsci: Selections from the cultural writings*, ed. D. Forgacs and G. Nowell-Smith; trans. W. Boelhower (Cambridge: Harvard University Press, 1991, p. 417).

10. It helps us to think of events as having "totalities" in order to explain the incompleteness and seemingly infinite perfectibility of our accounts of them. Nevertheless, given all of the constraints involved both in reporting events and in learning from those reports, and their different levels of civic relevance, it is sometimes useful to call some accounts "complete," particularly if they report the first "4 w's": who, what, when, and where.

11. D. Remnick, "Reporting it All: A.J. Liebling at One Hundred," *The New Yorker*, March 29, 2004: p. 57.

12. M. Safer, on the PBS program *Reporting America at War* Nov. 17, 2003.

13. S. Freedman, *Letters to a Young Journalist*; pp. 58-59.

14. (Ahab): H. Melville, *Moby-Dick*, Ch. 35 ("The Quarter-Deck).

15. For example, every Anglophone journalist would do well to read George Orwell's classic essay, "Politics and the English Language."

16. For a philosophical discussion of these issues see R. Bambrough, "Aristotle on Justice: A Paradigm of Philosophy," in Bambrough, ed., *New Essays on Plato and Aristotle*. London: Routledge & Kegan Paul, 1965. Another form of complexity incorporates the dynamic nature of time and causality, and may be defined as a limited number of things or features interacting to produce unpredictable results: e.g., the relatively simple rules of chess lead to complex games and strategies.

6

News and Ideology

Politics, like science, depends on our ability to persuade
each other of common aims based on a common reality.
                    — **Sen. Barack Obama, The Audacity of Hope**

I. News and Values

We began this book by observing the basic connections between
news and democracy: a two-way relationship if ever there was
one, because news without its democratic function is a mere
curiosity (and a mere commodity), and democracy without news
is inconceivable. So news is first of all a human value, both as a
commodity and (together with education) as an essential fuel of
the democratic process. It is not some kind of mineral ore waiting to be extracted, but the result of a labor-intensive process of
gathering and ordering information.

   The value of news, like other human values, is a bit complicated: like everything else, news is valued in different ways and
degrees by different people. Most values, like subatomic parti-
cles, are moving targets: fluid, and hard to measure or explain,
but also hard to avoid if we want to explain basic things,
because they permeate human relationships and institutions.
Journalism is no exception. Indeed, no human utterance or
communication, not even a smoke signal or a semaphore, can
be wholly "value free," inasmuch as there is some purpose or

motive behind it. Journalism is never wholly value free; unlike the weather, it has a purpose.

This does not mean that we do not need notions of truth and objectivity; only that, as we have seen, they have their limits. (To confuse matters, objectivity itself is a value — the value of being value free; and facts have value in the sense that knowing them advances our separate or joint purposes.) In this chapter, we will consider some of the problems that political values — values that by definition we do not all share — pose for journalism and vice versa. Here again, we are not proposing a remedy for these problems, just a bit of exploratory surgery in the hope of better understanding them, knowing that no journalistic vaccine awaits discovery.

Given the limited scope of cognitive objectivity (certainty in the absence of choice), the notion of easy objectivity, and of the journalist as an innocent harvester of neutral facts in a world before the ideological Fall, would seem inadequate and naïve. No perfect sand castle of facts can be built to withstand all subjective tides. But if journalists are compelled to make subjective choices, however guided by common sense, can they still hew to a standard of objectivity in the political sense, as a kind of neutrality? Or does such neutrality also represent an Innocence Fallacy, or an evasion of responsibility for the choices journalists actually make and their moral or political ramifications? If news is a democratic value, and thus presumably of some use to all citizens, where do news values intersect or collide with political values? That is the Pandora's box we are peeking into here.

Ideology per se is not the problem; it is the matrix of all political value, a force field that swirls around our every social act and social thought. As noted in Chapter 1, we have ideological differences because we have different interests, opportunities, and goals. More pointedly, capitalism generates inequalities that ensure that we have different interests and values, while history, religion, ethnicity, and personal circumstances further complicate those inequalities. Democracy is how we negotiate those differences and decide which ones should be neutralized by government and to what extent. Ideology is as natural and wholesome as democracy itself, and so is journalism. The problem is the uncertain no-man's-land between shared factual knowledge and the battleground of political values.

2.   Facts, Inconvenient Facts, and Values

Facts are notoriously "stubborn": they are more or less irrefutable, at least until new facts replace them. They are what we must agree on — or rather, what we come to agree on through shared observation, research, communication, etc. — if we are to agree on anything at all. Even definitions and linguistic conventions are facts of a kind, enabling imperfect communication to occur. We cannot discuss immigration reform, for instance, if we do not agree that Mexico lies immediately to the south of the United States, and also agree on what we mean by "immigration" or "south."

But if facts are absolutes of a kind (even trivial ones as in the above example), any claims that they represent more general truths must carry some qualifications. For one thing, facts change, sometimes more rapidly than "fact-finding" agreements about them can keep pace. Second, it takes time (and resources) to come to agreement on what the facts are; they do not just plop into our laps when they ripen. They must be found and shared.

Third, facts are at least partly relative, although seldom to a degree that renders them useless. They are unstable or relatively stable communities of agreement about the world. If you believe the earth is flat, then it is flat for you and like-minded thinkers, though round for everyone else. (You might still benefit from satellite communications, while remaining in denial; but you won't be ready to appear on *Jeopardy!*) Fourth, agreed-upon facts are subject to different interpretations. We may see the same dots but not connect them in the same ways. And unlike raw facts, the ways in which we connect those facts, the contexts and the frames into which we fit them, are very often (if sometimes obscurely) value laden.

Even the criteria for selecting or identifying facts are normative. Facts alone, outside of any possible context, are meaningless. If they seem to have meaning, it is because we implicitly supply the context. Putting facts in context, consciously or otherwise, invariably makes room for different ideas, habits of mind, interpretive styles, and so forth, which in turn relate to underlying worldviews, belief systems, and ideologies. Even "bare facts" cannot be contemplated free of any such biases; if they are not random, then they reflect some selection bias.

Ideally, factual considerations should determine which policies, strategies, tactics, and messages we use to achieve our political ends and thus to advance our values. To act rationally is to recognize what is real, insofar as we can, before trying to alter that reality. Rationality in this sense is mostly about the selection of optimal means. But while facts may delimit what is possible, in a particular time and place, they do not determine which ultimate goals and values we pursue, nor do they generate those values, or reconcile our value differences.

Least of all do facts render values irrelevant or unimportant. If anything, the higher the principles or more general the values, and the more removed from the grubby search for means to our ends, the less mutable or subject to revision they are on the basis of particular factual conditions. Okay, I might not go shopping today because of the fact that the weather is bad. But facts do not alter or disqualify basic life goals or ideals, unless those goals or ideals are utterly delusional.

Facts, and empirical generalizations from facts, help us to delineate the important boundaries of what is possible or foreseeable in a specific place and time; they identify limits on politics, democratic or otherwise. What was politically possible in South Africa in 1990 was not the same as in 1930 or 1960. But facts alone do not dictate what is good or fair or beautiful or conceivable. And of course, over time and with a bit of human agency, those factual conditions change.

Democratic citizens share certain basic values, more or less, while disagreeing ideologically. We share the ship of state but argue for different courses, and take turns at the helm. Our ideologies are democracy's pre-existing political conditions, so to speak: ways of organizing experience around competing ends. They are not subject to revision, embarrassment, or ridicule merely on the basis of facts. A conservative president invaded Iraq in 2003, but one can approve or disapprove of the decision to go to war without endorsing or indicting conservatism. With exceptions for extremes of militancy or intolerance, indicting basic values — as against simply opposing them — is more like indicting democracy itself.

But if factual conditions cannot ultimately embarrass democratic values, from time to time they do have a way of being terribly inconvenient to particular ideological agendas or arguments. This is an important paradox to keep in mind, especially in the heat of political arguments. It speaks to the ways in which we select, interpret, and deploy facts in our arguments, for our own legitimately partisan purposes.

Core political values are not formed out of facts, but out of ideal conceptions of the relationships between government, society, and the self. And moral and political disputes are not resolved by appealing to facts; if that were so, our differences would be continually reconciled as the facts came to light and were validated. (Likewise, in the courtroom, facts are supposed to determine whether a particular law applies — whether or not it has been broken — but not how to interpret the law, or whether it is a good law.)

Thus, agreements about facts rarely settle interesting arguments (except perhaps in science; and even there, competing interpretations must be debated); they are merely the shared understandings on which those arguments are based. Factual disagreements tend, rather, to freeze arguments until the facts can be determined. Facts never settle basic value differences, or cause people to abandon their commitments, though they may limit the attainability of certain ends or the ways of pursuing them. Arguments about what "the facts" are can presumably be decided empirically, but interpretations of them cannot; and arguments about values — well, in most cases they are never really decided. We invariably come away from such arguments with the same values we brought to them. Our values evolve slowly, and we are seldom talked out of them.

As nodes of consensus, then, facts are where we start from if we are to argue at all. They make it possible to conduct those debates in a common language. Particular facts may threaten or impoverish particular tactics or means to our ends; facts have a way of being unwelcome nuisances to some contentions or agendas and supportive to others. But they do not impugn basic democratic values.

In a communal enterprise, such as repairing a bicycle or constructing a nuclear device, people may share knowledge of certain facts in order to advance the project, or they may argue over the best way to get the job done; but presumably they agree in principle about what the job is. Pure science, and much applied science as well, requires no ideological qualifications; it is about manipulating nature to get from point A to point B, or from state A to state B. But as soon as we introduce the questions, Why B? Why not C? Why anything? And what if it affects X or Y? — that is, as soon as we interrogate *ends* — we open the Pandora's box of moral-political dispute. Journalism does not pop out of that box; it just has a way of prying it open.

The no-man's-land between ostensibly "pure" facts and values is a shadowy place lacking clear boundaries, and is difficult to map; that is because our values (like all conscious states) are themselves diverse, unique, often ineffable and vaguely defined amalgams of personal experience, psychic needs, and cogitation. These values form gradually, based on inchoate emotional and moral relationships between the self and the world. Ideological agendas and arguments, while rooted in such values, are coated with protective factual assumptions and generalizations, and so are more vulnerable to embarrassment when other facts or assumptions challenging our own (but not the values themselves) come to light.

It would be impracticable for our politics to become fact free and devolve into purely philosophical arguments. But philosophical arguments are exactly what they are, when you strip away the facts. We implicitly defend our basic values against competing ones whenever we argue; but we also need to confront the facts that exist, insofar as we can agree upon them, in order to try to solve the problems that confront us, as families, communities, or nations, however irreconcilable the different solutions.

More often, rather than ascending to the level of philosophy or political theory, our debates swing toward the opposite extreme, descending into polemic or into a zone of pseudo pragmatism that denies the normative dimension. We are urged to venerate practicality and bipartisanship, as if partisanship were something distasteful or unhygienic. Politicians are the worst purveyors of pseudo pragmatism, but journalists peddle it as well, because it avoids the nasty business of mucking around with conflicting values and goals. Pseudo pragmatism presumes that all we ever do is repair bicycles and build nuclear devices, and that we never need to have those undignified arguments about who gets what or why.

So we need facts in order to have democratic political debates, even if they sometimes complicate those debates; and we need journalists to supply those facts and put them in context, knowing that even context can put us on slippery political terrain. Context involves choices, frameworks, and habits of mind that cannot be wholly segregated from our value systems. These conspire to make journalism more complicated and messier than mere fact-mongering. The news is not the phone book.

Once we agree on the relevant facts, we can have open, informed debates about our ideological differences. (Admitting ideological considerations into the process of selecting — or ignoring — facts evokes the vulgar connotation of "ideology" as a kind of systematic ignorance.) Yet questions remain: which *are* the relevant facts, which are the most important, and how should we interpret them? It would be naïve to suppose that these questions can be decided entirely on neutral ground. And there is also the question of conscious bias.

There are two main reasons why factual information may be intentionally slanted (distorted, selected, or suppressed): subordination to economic interests (profit), and subordination to political interests (ideology). A third reason, often combined with the other two, is the simple urge to acquire or retain political or economic power. On the interpersonal level, other dark motives may be involved, rooted in psychological needs. To the extent that information is insulated from any such influences (a subject we shall examine in Chapter 8) it is more credible and useful to democratic citizens.

3.   The Uses of Neutrality

Democracies are systems for expressing and resolving conflict, not for suppressing or denying it. The left-right ideological spectrum explains and organizes such conflict systematically, if not completely, broadly reflecting the normal range of interest and opinion within a capitalist democracy. It is axial because most of our differences are expressible in relative terms vis-à-vis equality and freedom.[1] Other differences, such as those over social and moral issues, often align with views on equality.

An open society needs to have such normative arguments, and they cannot always be perfectly Socratic; hence, there must be advocacy journalism, a principal form of such argument. There are no clear boundaries (and no one with the authority to draw them) between philosophical debates about values and ideologically inspired selection or interpretation of facts. Reality is messy, and journalism is part of reality, as well as a principal means by which we perceive it — yet another paradox.

But if advocacy, in journalistic and other forms, is vital, there are also potential dangers in exclusive advocacy, that is, a media regime in which every fact is spun or interpreted to the left, right, or center. One such danger is intellectual dishonesty: for example, disregard of relevant but embarrassing or inconvenient facts. At the extreme, factual selectivity can become a form of polemic, which may inflame or polarize but offers little in the way of democratic glue. ("Here are the facts — the ones *I* like.") Having some factual common ground, while leaving plenty of room for contention, protects against those extremes.[2]

Rampant advocacy also discourages other instrumental values of civil discourse, such as critical thinking, candor, completeness, self-criticism, and the salutary effort to understand other points of view. Unchecked partisanship tends to keep company with weak arguments, bad-faith arguments, humbug, exaggerated and distorted factual claims, intolerance, denial, self-delusion, and general nastiness. General respect for the facts, and for critical thinking, can offset these tendencies and make advocacy more honest and robust.

Polarization is not just a question of how far apart people are, but also of how they are far apart. We want to limit our opponents' success, but not the very possibility of their success, because that would entail the failure of the whole democratic process of conversation, confrontation, and consensus. For that, we need factual common ground that only journalism within a culture of neutrality can supply. Thus, a vein of neutrality — at least of imperfect, aspirational neutrality — in the collecting, sorting out, and publicizing of relevant facts and narrative accounts of events is nearly as crucial to the democratic process as are advocacy and debate.

We need facts, along with stories and explanations and opinions, in order to focus and move the deliberative process. Facts are what bind us: common understandings that keep us from spinning off into separate, ideologically insulated tribes of pseudo citizens. There may only be a narrow range of issues (such as national security, or the need for a safe water supply) on which true nonpartisanship is possible. The point, however, is not to eliminate or reduce partisanship or to narrow the spectrum, but rather to contain it within a discursive framework conducive to consensus. Governments need thorough, objective (nonpartisan) intelligence-gathering in order to prosecute an effective foreign policy, regardless of which (value-driven) policies are chosen. In the same way, democratic citizens need a common flow of relevant, unbiased information about the world (along with other kinds), regardless of how they choose to interpret or use that information in their political lives.

We therefore need a "mainstream" of ostensibly neutral factual news, protected from the tributaries of advocacy, even if that mainstream is impossible to chart precisely, and always less than perfectly pure. Otherwise, we are merely talking to ourselves and those of like mind, and the public becomes more fractured — a mosaic of disconnected publics; think of how we are segmented already by cable TV or the Internet. We also need a critical culture to protect that mainstream from the ever-present threats of corruption or smuggled values. For example, news organizations that falsely claim to be "fair and balanced" erode the democratic common ground and also create a safe haven for absurdity and fatuity, which attracts unsavory creatures at the bottom of the journalistic food chain.

For similar reasons (and with similar qualifications), we need public educational institutions that unite us — or at least offer common ground on which to learn and debate — as well as institutions that express our divisions. There is a difference between hosting activism and institutionally promoting a particular point of view. It is not the mission of either the mainstream media or institutions of learning to foment activism or arguments of one stripe or another. It is part of their mission, rather, to encourage and facilitate activism and argument in general. "Institutions of learning are forums, not parties ..." writes Todd Gitlin. "So universities ought to embrace citizenship, not particular uses of citizenship."[3] A common curriculum, Gitlin adds, "enlarges the community of reason. It widens the circle of shared conversation."[4]

Granting the obvious need for partisan expression, much the same may be said of news. News aimed at balance and neutrality provides a fulcrum for real debate to take place, rather than a mere cacophony of contending voices. Part of the function of news is to be a "common curriculum" of current events.

Journalism, being more closely wedded to the flow of issues and events, tends, somewhat more than education, to find itself close to the ideological bone. That is part of its purpose. Neither education nor scholarship is a wholly neutral enterprise, free of ideological controversy. Beyond overt bias, many decisions — about facts, sources, quotes, or stories, the patterns to which they are related, the assumptions and ideas that frame them, the level of complexity at which they are communicated — bear at least a faint ideological signature.

Yet neither are these twin sectors of knowledge production hopelessly ideological. Different political cultures may govern different colleges and universities, as they do different news outlets. But while we have a (somewhat misleading) polarization of red states and blue states, we do not yet have distinct and rival red and blue cultures in news or in education. If we did, our democracy would be diminished. As much as we need ideological arguments for democracy to work at all, we need common ground in order to preserve civility and tolerance, maintain open communication, and achieve at least sporadic or temporary consensus.

That is not to say it is a simple matter. Objectivity qua political neutrality is not the same as objectivity qua epistemic certainty; it is a more complicated and vexatious notion, harder to identify and to obtain. For one thing, people are natural carriers of both conscious and unconscious biases; we are innately value-oriented creatures, with conscious aims far exceeding the survival instinct that we share with other animals. As we have seen, even putatively objective facts can tell slanted tales, depending on how they are selected, organized, and emphasized. How much neutrality is enough, and how perfectly neutral must it be? These are contestable if not imponderable questions.

4.   Problems of Neutrality

Beyond the critical but limited realm of relevant facts, there is a vast corona of possible communication that, even without any explicit ideological agenda, inevitably contains implicit or marginal biases. Such biases are informed by competing ideological views on a number of axes: equality versus inequality; the public sphere versus the private; interdependence versus personal independence; holistic versus positivist conceptual frameworks; simplicity versus complexity; the propensity to either legitimize or dismiss class; disparities or identities between appearance and reality; and so on. All of these are ultimately political vectors.

This coronal region is the Twilight Zone in which most journalism and education occurs: the region between objectivity and advocacy, in which we talk, argue, and observe without being either scientists or mathematicians, on one hand, or polemical advocates or mystics on the other. In this realm the production of knowledge can never be entirely free of political biases or agendas. Even hearing two sides of an argument is no guarantee that all the relevant facts will emerge, or that all the valid arguments or responsible points of view will be ably represented.[5]

Moreover, there are boundary problems in defining *mainstream, neutral,* and *news.* None of these terms can be defined with great precision or they would fail to reflect the realities of the world and of how we use language. News is too general a phenomenon not to overlap, at times messily or imperceptibly, with opinion, advocacy, propaganda, advertisement, entertainment — the gamut of communication genres. In the realm of words and images, nothing is ever completely immune to corruption or complication. Yet the civic mission of news makes it at least theoretically distinct from those other genres of communication, with their corrupting and complicating influences, and lends it a moral purpose and authority that they do not share.

A commitment to neutrality does not relieve journalists of responsibility for the ideological implications of how they frame or package the news. But neither can we hold them accountable for every possible inference or nuance as a disguised ideological time bomb. Conscious personal biases clearly do not belong in such journalism; yet anyone with no political biases whatsoever would probably do better to confine themselves to reporting about food or the weather.

Is all journalism, however neutrally inclined (and in the absence of conscious bias by journalists), susceptible to passive or structural biases? Perhaps no more so than education, in the absence of overtly biased teachers.

But here, at the risk of stating the obvious, two key differences between journalism and formal learning should be reiterated.

One is the predominantly commercial framework of news, at least in American society. Commercial news is self-evidently biased toward profit. But there are also subsidiary biases in content and coverage:[6] toward upscale consumers rather than other audiences; toward novelty and shock, sex and violence, and against reasoning, nuance, and detail; toward drama and personalities, and against groups or larger causal forces; toward strategy, and against substantive issues; toward simplicity and concreteness and against complexity and abstraction; toward the local or national and against the remote or foreign; and toward the near term and against the long term. Each of these is a signature of conservative bias. But more importantly, the profit motive is a dispositional bias against excellence, because for the most part, excellence does not pay.

A second significant difference between news and education relates to journalism's special role as a sponsor of political discourse. Schools and universities also sponsor political debate and activism, and would suffer if they suppressed it; but while they are loci of (mostly closed-circuit, semi-public) discourse, journalism broadcasts discourse to wider audiences and is quintessentially public. Journalism is not a training ground for democracy but a locus of it.

Other things being equal, both news and education are potentially progressive, equalizing forces in society, as well as stewards of vital democratic values. They are also potentially conservative, as forces for stability and memory, stewards of tradition, and arbiters of merit, decency, and expression. Both sectors disseminate knowledge that may yield political and economic empowerment to the individual citizen or consumer.

However, news equalizes more in the democratic sense than in the ideological sense: that is, in providing people with the intellectual and moral traction to be citizens, it is more of an equalizer of political than of economic power. Formal education, on the other hand, is a more structured and formative experience — typically an earlier one — and thus a more direct equalizer of status or wealth, providing particular traction in the economic realm. Again, this does not mean journalists do not have to worry about the political character of their work. Even when attempting to be neutral, journalism is a prism of political values and questions.

One facet of that prism is class. Democratic societies negotiate conflicts among competing and often unequal interests, economic and otherwise. A lot of journalism is about politics; and a lot of politics is about class. A prevailing cultural myth would have us believe otherwise: that "class warfare" is something unseemly, a hobgoblin of the left. Thus, how journalism treats, ignores, or suppresses issues of class, perpetuating or challenging prevailing ideas, is itself a highly political question, and another minefield for conscientious journalists.

Should journalism, in the often-quoted words of Peter Finley Dunne, "comfort the afflicted and afflict the comfortable"? It is hard to argue one way or the other without making a political argument. "Speaking truth to power" would seem to entail a kind of bias against the powerful; and surely it cannot be the role of journalism to speak up for the powerful and ignore the powerless. How do notions of balance, objectivity, and democratic neutrality square with compassion, empathy, or the inclination to side with the underdog? Contrarily, if the role of the "mainstream" is to remain as much as possible above (or beneath) the ideological fray, while hosting a wide array of ideological debate, does that mean that the less powerful citizens and institutions should be invisible?

Political bias assumes many forms and degrees, and we cannot afford to spend all of our time chasing its shadows. How much bias one sees is itself at least partly a political question. Bias is less of a problem in terms of particular stories or journalists — instances of conscious individual slanting — than in the broader patterns of story selection and treatment: in particular, in terms of the types of stories, frames, and sources that are *not* adequately represented.

There is no neutral Archimedean standpoint from which all bias is rendered visible, such that everyone can agree on where the bias lies. But that still does not entitle us to embrace a naïve belief in easy neutrality. Nor does it mean we should give up on neutrality altogether and allow commercial and political forces free rein. Freedom, justice, and independence are never achievable in absolute terms either, but that does not mean we do not pursue them.

Journalistic neutrality is, in the end, a problematic but important goal. Neutrality and commitment each have a place in the moral universe of democratic communication, as well as a fraught boundary. Two things justify this conflicted and qualified conclusion. One is a robust culture of media criticism to minimize and to police the gap between what we can achieve and perfect neutrality, by pointing out lapses or biases in ostensibly nonpartisan journalism. The other is the lack, in an angel-free media environment, of any better alternative.

Vexatious boundary questions remain: Where exactly are the proper boundaries of the "mainstream," and what counts as "political"? If political neutrality is a democratic value, how broad a "mainstream" is broad enough? What, beside the vagaries of the marketplace, is to prevent that mainstream from disappearing altogether — perhaps beneath a tide of ranting advocacy inspired by commercial or religious zeal? And can democracies rely for their basic information needs on the vagaries of the market?

A democratic conception of journalism must make room for a full range of expression and criticism. It must view with skepticism both the tendency to dismiss or ignore claims about ideology, on one hand, and on the other, countervailing claims that ideology so permeates news and knowledge production that no "facts" can usefully be said to exist. Philosophers might argue for this view and stay in business, but journalists cannot. Least of all does limited or qualified democratic neutrality justify the smug philistinism typical of the commercial mainstream, which wrongly equates neutrality with the political center; or the equally wrong-headed notion that being criticized from both sides of the spectrum represents some sort of validation; it is not that easy. One thing is clear: if you want perfect neutrality, tune in to the Weather Channel.

5.   Journalism and the Politics of Complexity

Should the news reflect the world (using the term *reflect* loosely of course) in all its complexity, as perceived by the journalist, or should it simplify for the sake of clarity or to reach a wider audience at a higher level of comprehension? The answer to this question is partly a function of how the journalist or news organization perceives that audience; and in a commercial context that perception is usually governed by the aim of maximizing audience (either numerically or in terms of purchasing power). But from the standpoint of excellence, there are intellectual and moral arguments for presenting the news with either more or less complexity. The complication is that complexity itself has a political footprint.

Generally speaking, more complex views of the world reinforce the values and arguments of the left, and simpler ones reinforce those of the right. Stepping down a rung on the ladder of abstraction, we might substitute *equality* for *complexity*. In every way, the left is more egalitarian than the right.[7] Making a society more egalitarian is a more complicated task — and one that assigns a more complicated role to government — than leaving things alone (laissez-faire). At one level, the simplicity of conservatism is reflected in its minimalist approach to politics and belief in small government.

At another level, conservatives make simpler assumptions about causality, favoring an existential view in which the individual is largely responsible for his or her destiny. Progressives implicitly assume a more complex causal scheme, giving weight to causal influences at various levels beyond the individual — the extreme case being the historical materialism of Marx, with its elaborate causal determinism.

Other axes, subsumed within the complexity-simplicity spectrum, further explain how we organize the world in left-right terms. The inclination to see connections as well as distinctions; to see the world in holistic rather than in partitional terms; to look for root causes and motives; to see discrepancies, rather than identity, between appearance and reality; to tolerate ambiguity: all of these habits of mind are more typical of the left, and differentiate us along the political spectrum.

These broadly opposing tendencies toward complexity and simplicity are obviously relative, definable in terms of one another; and both tendencies have their virtues as ways of understanding and communicating reality. Neither is demonstrably better or more correct; basic values are always contestable. Complexity and simplicity are also complementary virtues in the overall economy of meaning. How much we want to communicate, and how complex a message we wish to convey, must be weighed against the communicative advantages of simplicity, such as the time and effort required to formulate the message, and the extent and immediacy of comprehension on the receiving end.

Even when striving for neutrality, journalism — often without knowing it — acquires subliminal political overtones, leaning one way or the other within these force fields. In the mass media, particularly in electronic and tabloid media and in daily journalism, the more common leaning is toward simplification. Analysis, explanation, and context are almost by definition more complex, involving a search for causes, motives, interests, consequences, underlying distinctions, and connections: in short, for whatever is not apparent or obvious in the story and thus underscores the disparities between appearance and reality.

If there is a passive or structural bias in the journalistic enterprise itself, it leans in different directions at different levels. Daily journalism and hard news reporting may be said to be biased toward appearances and against deeper knowledge. "The beat system," as two media scholars have noted, "... reduces daily journalism to the coverage of mere appearances."[8] Insofar as commercial forces influence news coverage, they reinforce this bias to the right. The powerful vectors of culture, business, and technology invite or compel journalists to keep the news simple, superficial, dramatic, sensational, and personalized. News is what sells; context, investigation, and documentary reporting are in relatively short supply. These vectors are thus checks against complexity and communal and egalitarian impulses.

However, journalism's watchdog function and investigative role tell another story, linking the democratic agenda with more progressive ideas. James W. Carey wrote, "There is a bit of the reformer in anyone who enters journalism. And reformers are always going to make conservatives uncomfortable to some extent because conservatives, by and large, want to preserve the status quo."[9] (Conservatives may wish to change the status quo, but seldom in the direction implied by the word *reform,* of democratic expansion or renewal.)

Investigative reporting tends to underscore more complex and hidden realities, and so has a tendency to slant to the left. The intent to uncover deeper or more hidden truths, truths that require more digging than plucking, makes investigative reporting essentially more subversive and more revelatory than ordinary hard news. This puts it naturally at odds with powers that be and institutions whose interests lie in keeping such revelations from surfacing. Investigative journalism is also more focused on problems and the need for change; as Herbert J. Gans writes, "exposés have inherently reformist subtexts, and are thus hardly conservative ..."[10] Journalistic digging, either for facts that are hidden from public view or for deeper understanding of events, thus tends to produce a more complicated overall picture of social reality, and greater awareness of the disparities between how things appear and how they really are.

Journalists are understandably reluctant to acknowledge such biases, and they certainly are not uniformly progressive, viz., the conservative investigations of Bill Clinton.[11] But in general, in-depth reporting tends to correlate with wider distributions of responsibility, deeper and more intricate causal explanations, and a reality that is more at variance with appearance. These are not modes of inquiry one is likely to find at conservative think tanks.[12]

Journalism in a democracy must be a check on power, not a check on powerlessness. But that does not mean it must favor the outs against the ins. Solid reporting may affront any person or party. But insofar as the journalistic watchdog is a check on economic power, or the power of government in general — and particularly the power of government over the individual (as opposed to being a check on, say, organized labor or other nonprofit "special interests"), it is mainly a liberal check. Its bark tends to deter those seeking to contain democracy more than those seeking to expand it.

6. Excellence and Ideological Literacy

While reporting may be faulted for many reasons (not least for failing to provide the truth and nothing but), critiques alleging a partisan bias in the news are an important component of media criticism. Sometimes these claims are demonstrably valid; at other times they are mere political gamesmanship. What is important is the breadth and substance of the conversation about news and bias.

As we have seen, some of the ways in which news might be biased are quite subtle or even unavoidable; and some of those ways are themselves subject to dispute. Slanting or imbalance may be conscious or unconscious, and may involve the selection and presentation of news stories; the rendering of context or lack of it; choices of sources and quotes; the narrative texture, including wording and tone, emphasis, and overall framing. Focusing on the spectacular, the scandalizing, or the terrifying at the expense of nuance or complexity; using sound bites as substitutes for more complex discourse; reporting from the point of view of particular class interests, or suggesting that there are no class interests — all of these have political signatures.

In sum, political ideology is hydra-headed and endemic. It enters our discourse (including news) from all directions and in a variety of ways, virtually whenever we use language in public. Sometimes it is blatant, and sometimes a mere shadow, seen in the ways we communicate, of what we believe and how we wish the world to be. There is more than enough for political watchdogs to bark at.

Yet how vigilant we are, what we deem unacceptable, how shocked we are at ostensible betrayals of neutrality or truth — these too are fundamentally ideological responses (and properly so), and not the neutral reactions of a doctor to a disease. Critics are no more neutral than their targets. Conservatives typically cling more firmly to clear principles of objectivity and neutrality, in keeping with the positivism that celebrates appearances, and dismiss liberal accusations of slant in the corporate dominance of the media. Liberals and radicals, in keeping with their more complicated worldview, ascribe ideological biases that conservatives regard as phantoms. There is an occlusion, in other words, in assessing the role of ideology in the media: we invariably assess it through our own ideological lenses.

As the way in which we organize our political values, ideology is a complicated blend of personality, experience, and principle. If the media's mission is to inform and explain, and to support but not prejudge democratic ideological argument, the presence of bias is a matter of joint concern for journalists, media critics, and media-literate citizens. If bias cannot be avoided, with some critical sophistication it can at least be recognized and deflected.

What then can we fairly expect of journalists? Certainly not that they be constant and astute political critics of their own work and others'; that is too much to ask. We can expect mainstream journalists to avoid conscious slanting and to strive for balance and fairness, however imperfectly attainable (or definable). But more than that, we can expect that, whatever their personal biases, or the biases of their institutions or their particular media, they exhibit a certain ideological literacy, or critical political thinking. This means several things:

First, recognition that journalism is seldom ideologically pure or neutral, and that non-neutrality can assume many forms short of overt advocacy: in terms of assumptions, frames, the selection of stories, facts, sources or quotes, the level of complexity or explanation, etc. Journalists, more than anyone except teachers and scholars, need to be self-critical to achieve excellence. Media critics can help.

Second, ideological literacy means respect, not contempt, for the range of tolerant political viewpoints. They should be regarded as valid and intrinsic to the democratic process, rather than depraved or annoying. Dignified political argument should not be dismissed as "partisan bickering," and partisanship should not be confused with pettiness. To suppose that we can get on with the people's business and find consensual solutions without political debate, as if it were merely a matter of constructing bombs or bicycles, is naïve in the extreme. Ideological literacy means carefully distinguishing between neutrality, political centrism, and disdain for ideology.

Third, journalists should not only dignify but seek to understand the nature and roots of ideological differences, at least as representing differences about equality and morality. We should not dismiss the political arguments of the left as "class warfare," as if class were not the very basis of most ideological differences, just as we do not dismiss those of the right as "elitism," or denigrate arguments for racial equality as "race warfare."

Fourth, journalists should examine the political "frames" of the left, center, and right (as George Lakoff argues) to show how those frames color their contributions to democratic debate. Patriotism, for example, is not the exclusive property of the left or the right, and neither is faith, moral rectitude, or concern for national security, the environment, or the underclass. Journalists need to be critical thinkers about politics, as well as about everything else. As Lakoff writes, "… [I]t is the *special duty* of reporters to study framing and to learn to see through politically motivated frames, even if they have come to be accepted as everyday and commonplace."[13]

Fifth, journalists should exhibit a decent detachment from all powerful institutions, including corporations and government. They should not refer to the United States as "we" except to denote the American people, least of all in wartime, lest they abdicate their role as an independent check on power. Cheerleading is counterproductive to democracy.

It is sometimes the journalist's job to simplify, and sometimes to convey complexity, but never to unduly complicate; and given the trade-off between depth of understanding and the clarity and reach of simpler messages, it can sometimes be argued either way. But to venture very far in either direction is to leave political footprints. No one is perfectly neutral or free of bias; and the boundaries between intellectual biases or habits of mind and political leanings are opaque at best. The world does not conform neatly to our ideals — not even to the complicated ideal of neutrality. Between left and right, as between night and day, there is considerable twilight in which we chase our separate phantoms.

However, if some journalistic institutions did not devote themselves to an ideal of political neutrality, and thus form a "mainstream," if only by default, journalism cannot serve its key democratic purpose of generating factual accounts as foundations for partisan debates. We would end up instead with red news and blue news, and less common ground. Journalism at its best, like education, provides the building blocks for moral and political awareness, rather than actively shaping it.

Endnotes

1. As noted in Chapter One, without the inequalities of status, interests, and resources generated by capitalism (or any system short of totalitarian) there might arguably be no occasion for ideological differences, at least on economic questions; but as long as we have such differences, we need to express them and at least try to reconcile them, if only in the short run and on particular issues, through the democratic process.

2. Documentaries such as Michael Moore's *Fahrenheit 9/11* are highly selective, but are mainly comprised of responsible advocacy journalism, coupled with obvious polemic. Such unflattering portraits of political figures are once-sided but not necessarily unfair, or even misleading, because the polemical commentary and the actual reportage are clearly distinct and transparent.

3. Gitlin, *The Intellectuals and the Flag*, pp. 113-114.

4. Gitlin, op. cit., p. 115.

5. A "responsible point of view" might perhaps be defined as one which values truth but recognizes its limits in settling matters; values controversy and welcomes alternative perspectives but also recognizes controversy's limits in settling matters; and tolerates value differences without limits on such tolerance other than public safety.

6. For similar lists see: T.E. Patterson, "The United States: News in a Free-Market Society," in R. Gunther and A. Mughan, *Democracy and the Media: A Comparative Perspective*; and Scheuer, *The Sound Bite Society: Television and the American Mind*.

7. This is not to disparage either. It is a fact, which makes it possible for us to talk about "left" and "right" and make sense of our value differences, regardless of where we stand.

8. J. Ettema and T. Glasser, "On the Epistemology of Investigative Journalism," *Communication* 8:2 (1985): p. 189.

9. Carey, quoted in B. Cunningham, "Re-Thinking Objectivity," *Columbia Journalism Review* (July-Aug. 2003): p. 30.

10. Gans, *Democracy and the News*, p. 141.

11. There is a difference, of course, between looking for deeper structural explanations of events that contradict appearances, which is prototypically an enterprise of the left, and simply digging up whatever facts may indict or embarrass one's political opponents, which is a sport of both the left and the right.

12. There is a limited exception to this principle: conservatives sometimes argue that the complexity of the world as they find it is a reason to reject liberal policies. They argue, sometimes with great cogency, that such policies end up having unintended effects. But this is a limited and even opportunistic use of the notion of complexity, not one that is built into the conservative value system.

13. G. Lakoff, *Don't Think of an Elephant: Know Your Values and Frame the Debate — The Essential Guide for Progressives*. pp. 50-51 (italics added).

7

Ink and Ivy

The Curious Case of Journalism Education

> Journalism is, or ought to be, one of the great and
> intellectual professions.
>
> **— Joseph Pulitzer, in a 1902 memorandum**
> **proposing the Columbia School of Journalism**

I. Excellence and Education

Excellence, journalistic or otherwise, is (like freedom and other
abstract values) an important yet curiously vacant and formal
idea. Its meaning is derived from a context: the standards of a
given enterprise. It is a concept of value that attaches to other
values; except as a vague general idea, there is no such thing
as excellence as such (although there are common ingredients,
such as intelligence, diligence, or creativity). Thus, excellence
in journalism has nothing directly to do with excellence in
musicianship or navigation. No one endorses mediocrity —
although many achieve it. Almost by definition, mediocrity is
the norm, and excellence the exception. But what we mean by
excellence depends on the value or subject matter at hand.

Ideals of excellence exist to raise standards of human
achievement, or at least to keep us from slipping toward chaos
or depravity. But the conscious pursuit of excellence is also a
mark of excellence: it furthers the achievement both directly
and by example. For excellence to be achieved generally, it
must also be part of a culture, one among a pantheon of sus-

taining ideals. This means striving to perfect individual performance, and the structure and performance of institutions; but it also means training individuals to the profession's standards, and passing norms of excellence to rising generations. Which brings us to the unhappy, but hardly uninteresting, state of journalism education.

In most professions, if not in most human enterprises, standards of excellence are contextually apparent; it is part of the meaning of a "profession" that such standards are recognized and encouraged. And in most professional fields (unlike activities such as smuggling or prostitution, where practice makes perfect), the pursuit of excellence is inseparable from the acquisition of skills or knowledge, which are the natural purview of educational institutions.

The question of how to educate journalists is therefore central to the larger problem of journalistic excellence. Journalism education is controversial and problematic, its history checkered, its very mission plagued by doubt and debate. Although better educated than their predecessors, journalists today remain wary of academia, and get little respect from scholars in return. Journalism schools have never found a satisfactory balance between practical skills training, which does not necessarily require or benefit from a university campus, and intellectual training, which does.

Accordingly, this chapter will consider the potential for journalism education to promote journalistic excellence. It is not a systematic survey of the journalism school landscape or a critique of particular institutions, but rather a thematic discussion of the role of journalism education in society, and how it might best serve the democratic values associated with journalistic excellence. As with other aspects of journalistic excellence, the baseline here is not the satisfaction of journalists, media executives, journalism educators, academic deans, students, or media theorists. It is what produces the best journalism for democratic citizens. That is why a century ago, before any journalism schools existed, Joseph Pulitzer called for a school at Columbia University that would "make better journalists, who will make better newspapers, which will better serve the public."[1]

If journalism is, as Vartan Gregorian asserts, a "quintessential learning profession,"[2] then journalists in the complex media universe we now inhabit (and in which news itself is increasingly embattled) must be trained not just as fact finders but as critical thinkers, researchers, analysts, and critics. To be sure, it is not all about book learning; Ida Tarbell, Damon Runyon, H. L. Mencken, and Ring Lardner were not hacks. To know and report the pulse of a community or neighborhood (or a sport or an art form), to interview ordinary people as well as newsmakers with curiosity and compassion, is a form of excellence. But journalism cannot be modeled solely on fact-gathering, any more than it can be modeled on scholarly discourse. Journalism is "education of the moment," but the moment has a rich contextual environment that gives it meaning. It may draw on knowledge found in libraries, laboratories, or research institutions, as well as in offices or taverns. Journalistic ignorance, on the other hand, obviously disserves the public. To cite a recent example: reporting on the media and the Iraq war, Michael Massing found that in Doha, Qatar, where the media were based,

> the [American] reporters knew very little about the Middle East ... [t]hey were unfamiliar with Arab history, the roots of Islamic fundamentalism, the resurgence of Arab nationalism, the changes in the regional balance of power since September 11. Particularly serious was their lack of knowledge of Arabic. They could not talk with Arabic speakers directly, read Arabic newspapers, or watch Arabic news channels.[3]

2. The Strange History of Journalism Education

If the need for some kind of journalism education seems obvious enough, applying that insight has never been simple. The idea of journalism as a profession, with distinctive educational needs, emerged in the nineteenth century, along with technological advances such as the telegraph, the rotary press, and mechanical typesetting, as well as modern department stores and the mass-circulation commercial newspapers they supported.

The first unrealized plans for journalism education in America date from 1869, at Washington College in Virginia, and 1875 at Cornell University; the first curriculum organized around journalism was instituted at the Wharton School of Business in Philadelphia in 1893. The idea of an academic curriculum oriented to journalists emerged simultaneously in Europe.[4] Pulitzer, owner of the *New York World,* conceived the idea of a school of journalism at Columbia, in order "to raise journalism to the rank of a learned profession," spelling out his plan in an essay titled, "The College of Journalism" in the *North American Review* in 1904. A wealthy and respected news magnate (if not untainted by yellow journalism), Pulitzer had the radical idea that journalism, like education, was too important in a democracy to be left to the private sector:

> It is the idea of work for the community, not commerce, not for one's self, but primarily for the public, that needs to be taught. The School of Journalism is to be, in my conception, not only not commercial, but anticommercial.[5]

It took some years, however, for the outsized egos of Pulitzer and Columbia's president, Nicholas Murray Butler, to come to terms. In the meantime, the nation's first school of journalism was established at the University of Missouri in 1908. In the end, Pulitzer decided the school should not be launched until after his death, and so the Columbia School of Journalism finally opened its doors in 1912. It is widely considered America's flagship school of journalism.

From the outset, the school at Columbia was beset by questions about its mission. What began as a four-year liberal arts curriculum, designed to prepare undergraduate students for journalism careers, by 1919 had evolved into a two-year program for upperclassmen. Practice soon came to predominate over theory, as Columbia shed the high-minded ideals of its founder. Ironically, Pulitzer is better remembered not for the school that did not take his name, but for the unrelated journalism prizes that did, and which are administered in the same building.

In 1935, the Columbia journalism program was recast as a one-year graduate course, which remains intact (along with a recently added track involving an optional second year). When the one-year course was instituted, the *New York Daily News* commented, "We consider that a step in the right direction, but believe that the course is still one year too long." The school's relationship to the University administration has long been strained, and the newsroom model of journalism education in an academic setting remains controversial. It represents not just a conflict between practical-minded journalists and academia, but a basic cultural failure: the inability to see journalism and scholarship as complementary avenues of inquiry and truth-seeking for democratic citizenship.

In effect, journalism schools and departments have been whipsawed between the proponents of professional practice (including many journalism professors) and those advocating a more academic approach. Since the mid-twentieth century, many journalism schools have been yoked to larger schools of mass communication, which have a broader curriculum, often including the "persuasion-based communication goals"[6] of advertising and public relations. If anything, this colocation of journalism and communications programs has not bridged but in fact widened the gap of distrust between journalists and scholars. By some accounts, it amounted to the colonization of journalism education by an alien academic force.[7] At the same time, the more professional and practical orientation of other journalism schools (and their general lack of university support) has subjected them to pressures from the professional journalistic community — pressures more commercial than democratic in nature.

Criticism, not just of particular journalism schools but of journalism education as such, is a long-standing American tradition. Contempt for the concept was expressed early on by such august figures as Walter Lippmann, H. L. Mencken, and A. J. Liebling, himself a graduate of the Columbia School of Journalism. The Hutchins Report, surveying the state of American journalism in 1947, did not even deign to systematically examine journalism education. It is a striking omission. The report did not neglect the subject entirely, but included a single scathing passage that in many ways has stood the test of time:

> [I]deals and attitudes in the professions of law, medicine, and divinity are cultivated by the professional schools of those disciplines. They act as independent centers of criticism. The better they are, the more independent and the more critical they are. The schools of journalism have not yet accepted this obligation. With few exceptions they fall short of professional standards. Most of them devote themselves to vocational training, and even here they are not as effective as they should be. The kind of training a journalist needs

most today is not training in the tricks and machinery of the trade. If he is to be a competent judge of public affairs, he needs the broadest and most liberal education. The schools of journalism as a whole have not yet successfully worked out the method by which their students may acquire this education.[8]

Robert M. Hutchins himself had earlier denounced the vocational approach to journalism in his 1936 book, *The Higher Learning in America*; in 1938, he wrote an article titled, "Is There a Legitimate Place for Journalism Education? No!"[9] The Report did, however, include a substantive proposal for mid-career journalism education: "The type of educational experience provided for working journalists by the Nieman fellowships at Harvard seems to us to deserve extension, if not through private philanthropy, then with the financial assistance of the press itself."[10]

One of the most searing critiques of journalism education since the Hutchins Commission's came in a report by David Boroff for the Ford Foundation, which appeared in shorter form in *Harper's Magazine* in October 1965. "If journalism schools were to disappear tomorrow," Boroff wrote, "I do not think this would be a serious blow to American culture."[11] He later added, "In a surprising number of schools, the academic deans acknowledged that if they were starting from scratch, they would not include a school or department of journalism."[12]

Boroff urged, improbably, a "drastic reduction in the number of journalism schools and departments. There simply isn't talent enough to go around." He also offered some constructive suggestions, including "a system of rotating professorships with the best journalists shuttling back and forth between the media and the university." And he echoed the proposal of the Hutchins Report that programs for working journalists like Harvard's Nieman Fellowship should become more widespread. (To some extent they have.)

In an unpublished 1966 paper, Hutchins argued that the university had become a "service station" for the rest of society, when it needed instead to be "an autonomous thinking community," and to help to "fashion the mind of the age."[13] A similar charge has been made repeatedly against journalism schools; by and large, they are service stations for professional journalism rather than independent centers of critical thinking about media, journalism, and society. The idea of the school as a service station may be appropriate for some professions; however, the knowledge professions, which do not serve particular markets or constituencies but democratic discourse (and which play more complex political roles in society than, say, architecture, divinity, or accounting), require a more independent, critical approach: that of "autonomous thinking communities."

American journalism schools have never been centers of dissent or magnets for alternative views of the media, or much autonomous thinking. They are certainly not places where one is likely to find courses on critical media theory or discussion of media concentration. More than anything, they are a feeder system for the journalism profession. Their institutional conservatism is partly due to the sociology of the journalism profession, and partly, perhaps, a vestige of the era of their founding, when different notions of journalism, objectivity, professionalism, and citizenship prevailed. But it is not primarily a political conservatism, and criticism of j-schools is not confined to, or even closely identified with, the political left. Terry Eastland, publisher of the conservative *Weekly Standard,* writes:

> [T]hough journalists aspired to the status of professionals, they never acquired the self-regulatory mechanisms found in law, medicine, or even business. The nation's journalism schools, which taught — and still teach — a craft better learned on the job, never really filled the void. Those schools often tended to hire former journalists lacking both the intellectual capability and the inclination to undertake serious analysis of the institutions whence they came. Critical scholarship by those outside the guild tended to be summarily dismissed, and the field was always thin on professional journals and guiding ideas.[14]

Such harsh critiques, laced with charges of anti-intellectualism, have been made with regularity, including by some journalism professors. Jake Highton, writing in the journal of the National Conference of Editorial Writers in 1988, echoes Boroff and Pulitzer: "What journalism students need is an education — not a journalism education."[15] Highton adds, "A huge problem at J-schools is that the educators themselves lack depth, scope, and intellect." He quotes Ted Koppel's remark: "Journalism schools are an absolute and total waste of time. You cannot replicate true journalism — genuine pressure — in an academic setting."[16] Of course, the inability to "replicate true journalism" in an academic setting does not mean that there is nothing useful to be learned about journalism in schools, or that student newsrooms or broadcast studios have nothing to offer would-be journalists.

Yet, even those who instinctively balk at the idea that journalism and education have nothing to share are hard put to make a stronger case. "Where press and university meet should be a vibrant, beneficial juncture," wrote Douglas Birkhead in 1991, in one of the more thoughtful considerations of the problem.[17] Yet Birkhead was unable to locate that juncture precisely or give it meaning. More recently, the late James W. Carey, a leading communications scholar who migrated to the Columbia Graduate School of Journalism, noted with understatement that "the fit has always been a little uneasy" between journalism and the university.[18]

Overall, journalism schools exercise little influence over what is widely referred to as the "news industry." They tend to react to trends in the field more than influence them. They are seldom sponsors of independent criticism (the *Columbia Journalism Review* and the *American Journalism Review* being among the handful of important exceptions). Nor are they essential portals of entry for a journalism career. And the debate over whether to focus on practical skills or academic knowledge grinds on.

Among the 450-odd departments and schools of journalism in the United States (of which only a hundred or so are accredited), there are wide disparities in quality and orientation. In many schools, journalism is taught at the undergraduate level, arguably displacing more important foundational learning in the liberal arts. Often there is little or no connection between a journalism school and the university's campus media.[19] As noted earlier, many schools commingle the teaching of journalism with advertising and public relations, which are not notably devoted to the disinterested pursuit of truth or the civic weal.

If journalism schools in their present form were to disappear, the nation would not suffer. Any void would be filled by some combination of academic study, campus journalism, and internships. The fact that enrollments continue to rise, even as mainstream news outlets lose audience and cut their staffs, is hardly proof that j-schools are irreplaceable. They may do less harm than good, but the question is not who is harmed; it is rather, how can they be improved as institutions to foster excellence?

Before turning to that more constructive approach, we might note that professional schools in business, architecture, law, and most other professional and academic programs are not similarly plagued by a hostile stand-off between scholars and practitioners, isolated on their campuses, dictated to by their professions, or subjected to chronic calls for their demise. This is not simply due to the failure of journalism educators to play a leadership role, or their suspect academic credentials. It is more likely due to journalism's inherent generality and breadth, its derivative nature as a system for brokering knowledge, and its fragmented and partly subjective standards of excellence: because the skills it involves are diverse, somewhat inchoate, and not wedded to a particular knowledge base. One can be a good journalist by combining intelligence, a certain knack, and a good general education. Yet journalism and education, though not as clearly defined or as directly related to specific tasks or bodies of knowledge, are (unlike most other professions) critical to the functioning of a democracy.

It is not accidental that similar critiques have chronically afflicted the other great knowledge profession. Graduate schools of education have experienced a parallel dilemma between practical skills and academic knowledge.[20] In both fields, the need for high professional standards is clear; both serve broad public constituencies, rather than addressing specific needs of shifting minorities. Both lack a single knowledge base, and rely on practical skills as well as breadth of knowledge, although both also have niches in which specific expertise is necessary or desirable. And in both fields, undergraduate concentration is arguably inimical to the broader liberal education that, with rare exceptions, spurs practitioners to excel.[21]

Furthermore, teachers and journalists alike, despite decades of professionalization through graduate programs, research institutes, journals, unions, etc., are lower in social standing and income than other professions. Yet teachers and journalists are more directly important to the practice of democracy than other professionals who have higher incomes and status or more advanced training, because their purpose is to empower citizens civically, culturally, and economically. Language is part of the problem. The term *profession* creates a boundary that is too simplistic and severe.[22] If journalism and teaching are not professions in the sense of engineering or dentistry, neither are they "crafts" in the same sense as basket-weaving.

The Columbia Graduate School of Journalism has recently embarked on a new path, evolving in a more academic direction without eliminating the newsroom model. In mid-2002, Lee C. Bollinger, newly installed as Columbia's president, abruptly called off a nearly completed search for a new journalism dean, and formed an elite task force to examine the mission of journalism education. The group issued no formal report; a relatively brief statement was issued in the spring of 2003 summarizing the discussions.

At a meeting with alumni of the Journalism School in April 2003, Bollinger said that Columbia was looking for "the right balance between engagement with the world and removal from the world." Echoing the comments of both the Hutchins Commission in the 1940s and David Boroff in the 1960s, Bollinger expressed interest in the idea of fellowships like the Nieman program at Harvard, which brings working journalists to the campus for periods of academic study. (Various mid-career programs financed by foundations have been offered at Columbia since the 1960s.) His speech drew groans from many in the audience.

Later that year, Nicholas Lemann, a member of Bollinger's task force who had spelled out a bold vision for the intellectual renewal of journalism education, was selected to lead the school. Soon after, Columbia inaugurated an optional second year of study, leading to a master of arts degree, adding an academic year to the traditional one-year program of training and study, with four areas of possible concentration — politics, the arts, business, and science. Perhaps Lemann, with Bollinger's support, can finally steer Columbia toward Pulitzer's founding vision.

3.   A Cautious Case for Journalism Schools

Despite a century of failure to balance practical and academic training, or to find a stable home within the university, journalism education is unlikely to be abolished. More than that, abolition would represent the abdication of Joseph Pulitzer's core idea — even more radical in his day than in ours — that journalism is civically and intellectually important. It is not just a system of fact-farming requiring its own sharecroppers, but a complex process of gathering, organizing, criticizing, and diffusing knowledge. As such, it is naturally kindred to scholarship and warrants a vital connection to universities.

What can be said in favor of American journalism schools as presently constituted? A weak prima facie case can be built around rising enrollments and the often positive testimony of alumni who feel they have been well served. At worst, journalism education in its present form represents a lost opportunity (both for universities, as a misallocation of their resources, and for society as an imperfect system for training journalists). And, whatever the quality of the learning experience, important peer education no doubt occurs in an educational setting that would be hard to replicate elsewhere.

However, satisfaction of market demand begs the question of whether alternative institutions, or different orientations in existing ones, would better serve society. Arguably, institutional inertia sustained by stable constituencies — such as students eager for a credential, professors, retired journalists, and alumni — keeps j-schools alive in their current form irrespective of their utility to society as a whole. There is no evidence to suggest that journalism alumni are demonstrably better than other journalists. The author of one major study of journalism education, Betty Medsger, reports finding in a survey that 59 percent of print journalists who won Pulitzer Prizes, 75 percent of broadcast journalists who won DuPont Awards, and 58 percent of those awarded Nieman Fellowships never studied journalism.[23]

Traditional journalism programs may also have greater relative value for overseas students: not just as a cross-cultural experience, but to educate journalists from countries with less freedom of the press and weaker journalistic cultures. Other things being equal, these students may represent a better investment in democracy. In this connection, Sanford J. Ungar has suggested that leading American media organizations "sponsor and conduct practical training of journalists from other countries in the kind of hard-hitting, no-holds barred reporting that makes the press such an essential component of the democratic system in the United States … with schools of journalism and communication providing an academic framework where appropriate."[24]

Journalism schools may also have a positive effect in accelerating the integration of women and minorities into the media workforce. This is a good thing in itself, although American journalism is still a long way from "reflecting" the American population; and in education, as elsewhere, diversity must be weighed against competing goals.

The widespread hybrid curriculum, combining academic and practical training, is not on its face counterproductive to learning, merely suboptimal. Practical skills might be better learned through internships or at entry-level jobs, and j-school curricula might be more coherent; but j-schools are, on their own terms, centers of useful learning. If nothing else, the hybrid curriculum reflects a basic reality: journalists need to know both "how" and "what."

However, none of these considerations defeat arguments for change and experimentation. Rather, they suggest that Joseph Pulitzer's conception of journalism education had merit (especially once it migrated to the graduate level where it belongs), and has even more merit in a more complex and educated society. But — Columbia's and other experiments notwithstanding — it is hard to deny that the schools themselves have failed to evolve along with journalism and society; most remain stuck in the mid-twentieth century.

We need to recognize the natural intellectual connections between the "ink-stained" wretches of the digital era and their brethren in academia. Ironically, the failure of the journalism school idea partly represents the failure of journalists themselves (as well as educators) to imagine reporting as Pulitzer did: as a dignified intellectual and civic enterprise that is both distinct from and related to teaching and scholarly research.

4. News and Knowledge Revisited: Journalism and Scholarship

Times have changed, at least somewhat, since H. L. Mencken accused journalists of having "a widespread and almost fathomless prejudice against intelligence." Over recent decades, no other profession can claim more improvement in the overall education level of its members, despite certain vestiges of anti-intellectualism. In several obvious ways, journalism is altogether unacademic. It has a lay audience, and it is mainly about the here and now: new and often evanescent knowledge of a recent and public nature. As G. Stuart Adam observes,[25] journalism and scholarship

> generate distinctive forms of knowledge. Journalism is concerned with the recording of human experience as it occurs. The experience it presents is raw. It depends heavily on a vocabulary that is concrete and a grammar that is active. It eschews the abstract; it is open-ended. By contrast, scholarship is the product of sustained reflection on human experience. Formal scholarship is cooked and/ or distilled and it follows relatively strict methodologies.

Nevertheless, journalists and scholars also share certain essential concerns. One is a basic concern for truth: for facts as building blocks of knowledge. Both journalism and scholarship require accuracy and relevance — truths that are verifiable and important — as well as interpretation and argument. Both also go beyond facts to tell larger truths about the world, analyzing and dissecting, synthesizing and connecting, identifying and explaining, relating different levels of generality, and putting things into context.

The mutual wariness, if not outright hostility, between the parallel worlds of journalism and scholarship (and between journalism education and host universities) is based on old and natural fissures, including mutual jealousies and fears; but it disserves the wider public, and reflects a blinkered view of the dialectic between the ivory tower and the rest of the world. In some circles scholarship may enjoy a higher cultural status than journalism, but that is not saying much; and invidious comparisons do not help the search for common ground. (Nevertheless, word for word, journalistic writing is arguably more difficult than academic writing, yet the latter — despite its greater freedom from commercial and time pressures — is more often mediocre or obscure.[26] And if scholars are the guardians of civilization, journalists, generically, are the guardians of democracy.)

The gulf between scholarship and journalism is in any case unnaturally wide, and impoverishes all parties. The academy should be a resource for the rest of society, not an elite refuge from it. Its natural connections to journalism should be reflected in productive relationships. This means that journalists need to think and behave more like scholars, and scholars (especially those who study society) need to think and behave more like journalists.[27] The many points of tangency should be exploited collaboratively rather than ignored. James W. Carey, for example, noted the close connections between urban journalism and sociology.[28] It is not as if students never need journalism, and older citizens never need education. Our culture of pragmatism exalts doing above thinking, as if they were incompatible; but in mutual isolation, both are overrated. Journalism and scholarship must reject these antithetical cultural frames.

In fact, they should actively cross-pollinate. Antonio Gramsci, in his Prison Notebooks from the 1930s, proposed that informal schools of journalism be formed within newspapers;[29] that kind of training and mentoring is unlikely to happen in the present hyper-commercial news environment. Active participation in journalism, and collaboration with journalists, might enrich students and scholars in many fields, including history, politics, sociology, economics, business, and law, among others. The Hutchins Commission implicitly endorsed this notion of scholarly and student journalism (albeit with typical brevity and vagueness), remarking in passing that "educational institutions have a responsibility to use the instruments employed by the agencies of mass communications."[30]

In addition to bringing scholarly insights to a wider audience, such crossover could help to dissolve the cultural and professional barriers between journalism and scholarship, and help scholars to see the practical and civic implications of their own areas of learning. Herbert J. Gans has it exactly right:[31]

> Any program that teaches both journalists and fledgling scholars would be a blessing for both. Journalists might learn some analytic skills and the theoretical perspectives of scholars. The scholars, on the other hand, may become interested in the 'real world' topics that journalists write about and drop some of the intellectually

more dubious pursuits, as well as the jargon, constructed in the ivory tower. In time, the destructive miscommunication and the considerable hostility that now exist between the journalistic and scholarly communities might shrink and then disappear.

5. What Journalists Need to Know

There must be some useful academic preparation for a profession as important and complex as journalism. No curriculum can suit the needs of every would-be journalist, just as none can fit every would-be educator; this argues for flexibility and experimentation. Journalists, like scholars, formulate knowledge by knitting facts to contexts. They need analytic and critical as well as narrative skills and substantive knowledge. The intrinsically hybrid nature of journalism — its dependence on both concrete skills and broader knowledge — cannot be resolved in the abstract; there is no point of reconciliation between skills and knowledge waiting to be discovered. Subject knowledge and practical skills will always jointly affect the quality of reporting, just as they jointly affect the quality of teaching.

The problem remains both a practical and an intellectual one: what can journalists learn in an academic setting, and when and how should such study combine with or yield to the actual practice of journalism? The first question is the easier one: journalists should study whatever brings depth and sophistication to their work; without begging the question, that could be almost anything. Some forms of journalism require generalists, others demand expertise; specialization or expertise is what university campuses best provide at the graduate level, just as they provide breadth to undergraduates. Columbia's master of arts program aims to do that through its four areas of concentration; but why limit it to those? Why not offer, for example, a journalism track with a concentration in Arabic and Middle Eastern studies, or environmental science, or public health — or anything else of journalistic relevance?

A vast range of academic subjects are potentially of such relevance — including history, politics, law, economics, business, sociology, psychology, the sciences, technology, urban planning, regional studies, and languages. History is perhaps most relevant of all, especially to the generalist, given its intrinsic connections to journalism; but it does not hurt to be a polymath. A master's degree in any of these subjects would be more useful than a degree in journalism; better still, a master's degree with a concentration in journalism, similar to existing joint-degree programs.

In addition to the many areas of possible specialization, there is a well-defined core of academic subjects that are directly relevant to all journalists. These include media history, law, and ethics; "media and society," or the interpenetrations of media and politics; and (especially) rigorous media criticism. Thus, it would seem logical to divide a journalist's education into four parts or phases: undergraduate breadth in the liberal arts; graduate-level specialization; core media-related courses; and skills training.

6.   The View from Here

Based on the foregoing ruminations, I will conclude with some ideas for refocusing journalism education. There are two overlapping goals: first, and most important, to better prepare journalists to strive for excellence; and second, to encourage stronger bonds between journalists and universities. Refocusing, in this case, means both broadening and narrowing: broadening the basic conception of what journalism is, and how education can improve it and even blend with it, while providing more concentrated learning for individual journalists.

These ideas are intended to provoke further thinking, and may seem impractical, or merely disagreeable, to some journalists and journalism educators. But no study or task force can achieve for journalism education the dignity it aspires to, or silence its critics, if journalists talk only among themselves, inside the box, or without making common cause with scholars. The status quo reflects weaknesses in, as well as schisms among, academia, the journalism profession, and the wider democratic culture.

First, the newsroom model of skills training should be actively discouraged within the undergraduate curriculum, because it displaces more important learning. Campus journalism and professional internships should replace it.

Second, skills training should also be phased out of graduate journalism school curricula. J-schools should either eliminate the teaching of skills altogether — Stanford's journalism department has moved in this direction — or reconstitute it as a collaborative enterprise with campus or professional news media. Certain advanced courses, such as investigative and documentary journalism, should be retained along with the core media courses cited earlier (law, ethics, history, criticism, etc.), because like those courses they are important, fit naturally into an academic setting, and are difficult to replicate in the job environment.

An interim measure would be to confine practical training to intensive short courses involving work at a news organization; any supervised practicum or master's thesis should be for actual broadcast, Web posting, or publication. If my own experience as a journalism student taught me anything, it is that the kind of simulated newsroom training that constituted the bulk of a full academic year could easily have been condensed, leaving more time for core courses and specialization.[32]

A third improvement would be for journalism schools to de-credentialize their programs by not granting academic degrees, or at least not in journalism. Degrees do little or nothing for consumers of journalism (or for the profession, for that matter) and merely underscore the awkward and synthetic nature of journalism education. The academic degree system is unsuited to the differing and complex needs of modern journalists. (It is probably inappropriate to many other fields as well.) It radically simplifies and distorts the extent and depth of study, and the level of actual accomplishment, and ignores the disparate needs of different students. The degree functions as a kind of credentializing toll booth for career advancement and little else. Perhaps, instead, master's programs in the many fields relevant to journalism (as well as focused interdisciplinary programs) should be offered with journalism concentrations, including actual reporting and collaboration between academic departments and news organizations.

Fourth, more schools should implement the idea endorsed by the Hutchins Commission report, David Boroff's report for the Ford Foundation, and President Bollinger of Columbia, by offering short focused seminars on the Nieman Fellowship model to working journalists. This may be the single most overdue change: addressing the needs of working as well as prospective journalists. The different needs of recent college graduates, with and without campus journalism experience, and of journalists at various stages in their careers, call for flexible programs of differing types and lengths — and cast further doubt on the value of granting degrees. As Orville Schell observes, "journalism schools can … justify their existences by striving to become workshop-like places where older and more seasoned journalists team up with younger journalists to do actual projects that get published, aired or exhibited."[33]

Fifth, all journalism schools should strive to be independent centers of criticism and debate about journalistic issues and society (for which the Internet is an excellent vehicle), and should incorporate that critical spirit into their curricula. Students should learn by critiquing the work of their peers and the professional media, and should study the principles and history of media criticism.

Neither the practical or "newsroom" model nor a purely academic one is ideal for either the aspiring or the working journalist. What is needed is a more dynamic fusion of the two models, and one that is more flexible to the needs of particular individuals. Practical experience and intellectual knowledge both count toward excellence — along with curiosity, imagination, and courage. The ideal journalist, in short, is both well rounded and an expert. He or she will have a critical and skeptical temper, an understanding of the legal and moral parameters of the journalism profession, and a clear sense of its history, civic function, and critical standards.

Given the barriers that exist at present, exacerbated by the marketplace, it will require a paradigm shift to see journalism and education as taproots of the same democratic tree, and part of an information environment cohabited by citizens, journalists, and scholars. It will mean relaxing the boundaries, and perhaps the very definitions, of academic and journalistic institutions. But since knowledge abhors artificial boundaries, and cultural barriers only serve narrow constituencies, this will no doubt happen eventually.[34]

Finally, journalism schools can serve as laboratories for alternative models of both teaching and doing journalism — and alternative economic models — in keeping with Joseph Pulitzer's vision of journalism as "one of the great and intellectual professions." In the long run, there is great potential for synergy between j-schools, universities, foundations, and research centers, with or without the help of traditional news organizations. They can produce knowledge that is timely, relevant, and accessible to the public, but also free of commercial constraints, and enriched by society's deepest reservoirs of knowledge. That way points toward excellence.

Endnotes

1. Quoted in J. Boylan, *Pulitzer's School*, p. 251.
2. V. Gregorian, "Journalism, the Quintessential Knowledge Profession, has an Information Problem" www.journalism.nyu.edu/pubzone/debate/forum.
3. M. Massing, *Now They Tell Us: The American Press and Iraq*. NY: New York Review Books, 2004; p. 14.
4. For example, Karl Bücher's plan of studies at the University of Leipzig in the early 20th century: see *H. Hardt, Social Theories of the Press*, pp. 199 ff.
5. J. Pulitzer, Jr., "The College of Journalism," *North American Review* (1904).
6. See S.D. Reese, "The Progressive Potential of Journalism Education: Recasting the Academic versus Professional Debate," *Harvard International Journal of Press Politics* 4:4 (1999): p. 73.
7. "At mid-century," writes Betty Medsger, "a very significant change took place when the founders of communication studies as a distinct discipline chose journalism for its home. They moved rather swiftly to diminish the journalism part of their programs and soon eliminated experience and expertise in journalism as a qualification for teaching. This 'takeover' of journalism education as a way of creating a home for communication studies, whose scholars formerly had been dispersed among various disciplines ... greatly slowed the development of journalism education ... Communication studies, in much of its research, focused on learning to control the mass audience rather than on how to serve the information needs of citizens." B. Medsger, "Is Journalism Different?" www.mtsu.edu/~masscom/seig96/medsger/medsger.htm. See also: James W. Carey, "Where Journalism Education Went Wrong" www.mtsu.edu/~masscomm/seig96/carey/carey.htm.
8. Hutchins Report ("A Free and Responsible Press"), U. of Chicago Press, 1947; p. 78. An important later exception to the report's assertion would be the *Columbia Journalism Review*, founded at the Columbia School of Journalism in 1962, and arguably the leading venue for American media criticism.
9. Hutchins, *The Higher Learning in America*, p. 56; and *The Quill* (Vol. 26: March 1938).

10. (Nieman-type fellowships): "A Free and Responsible Press," p. 95.

11. D. Boroff, "What Ails the Journalism Schools?" *Harper's Magazine*, Oct., 1965, p. 78.

12. Boroff, op. cit., p. 87. Boroff elsewhere observed [p. 80] that, "It is revealing … That the best researchers into the mass media … are in research institutes which are not part of journalism schools." This is no longer as true as when Boroff wrote.

13. Hutchins, quoted in Dzuback, M.A., Robert M. Hutchins: *Portrait of an Educator*, p. 262.

14. T. Eastland, "Starting Over," *The Wilson Quarterly* (Spring 2005): 42-43. In notable contrast, the field of communications has literally dozens of academic journals.

15. J. Highton, "Perhaps it's Time to Abolish Journalism Schools," *The Masthead* (National Conference of Editorial Writers) (Winter 1988): p. 33. See also J. Merrill, *Existential Journalism*.

16. Highton, op. cit., p. 34.

17. D. Birkhead, "Journalism Education: Is There a More Meaningful 'There' There?" *Media Studies Journal* (Winter 1991): p. 121.

18. J. Carey, "Where Journalism Education Went Wrong," www.mtsu.edu/~masscom/seig96/carey.htm; p. 4.

19. One exception is the University of Missouri School of Journalism, which publishes both the Missourian, a daily newspaper co-produced by faculty and students in Columbia, MO, and also news for a local FM radio station and a TV station.

20. One difference is that schools of education have more often been accused of being overly academic rather than too practical. And journalism's peculiar Constitutional role relative to the First Amendment inhibits any forms of self-regulation or even of organization.

21. Samuel G. Freedman writes that "You don't need a class to teach you how to interview or report or construct a basic article if you have the opportunity to work on a high-school or college newspaper (or radio station, television station, or Web site). College should be your time of intellectual exploration, and, in my own case, I despair over every journalism class I took that could have been a class in political science or English literature or virtually anything else." (*Letters to a Young Journalist*, p. 137.)

22. I am grateful to James Boylan for this and many other helpful points.

23. B. Medsger, "Getting Journalism Education Out of the Way," www.journalism.nyu.edu/pubzone/debate/forum.1.essay.medsger.html. (Medsger is the author of *Winds of Change: Challenges Confronting Journalism Education*. Arlington, VA: Freedom Forum, 1996.)

24. Ungar, "The Role of a Free Press in Strengthening Democracy," in J. Lichtenberg, ed., *Democracy and the Mass Media*, p. 395.

25. G.S. Adam, "The Education of Journalists," *Journalism* 2:3 (Dec. 2001): 330-331.

26. "Increasingly," writes Richard Campbell, "academics partial to maintaining boundaries between specialized realms of knowledge are openly hostile to the clarity and simplicity of the kind of communal language represented by good journalism — language that has long served as the model for public intellectuals interested in communicating with peers in other disciplines as well as with the general public." ("Journalism is Different, So Let's Get Rid of It," www.mtsu.edu/~masscom/seig96/medsger/ campbell. htm.)

27. This is especially true for pundits, as Eric Alterman points out; see the Conclusion to *Sound and Fury: The Making of the Punditocracy*.

28. J. Carey, "Where Journalism Education Went Wrong," www.mtsu. edu/ ~masscom/seig96/carey.htm. "Journalism," Carey added, "naturally belongs with political theory, which nurtures an understanding of democratic life and institutions; with literature, from which it derives a heightened awareness of language and expression and an understanding of narrative form; with philosophy, from which it can clarify its own moral foundations; with art, which enriches its capacity to imagine the unity of the visual world; with history, which forms the underlying stratum of its consciousness."

29. Gramsci writes: "For certain types of newspapers the problem of the professional school must be solved in the newspaper office itself, by transforming or integrating regular staff meetings into organic schools of journalism. Young people and students from outside should be invited to attend lectures there along with the staff, so that eventually real politico-journalistic schools are formed, with lectures on general topics (history, economics, constitutional law, etc.) which might also be entrusted to competent outside experts who are able to take into consideration the needs of the newspaper." (A. Gramsci, *Selections from Cultural Writings*, ed. D. Forgacs and G. Nowell-Smith; Harvard U. Press, 1985; Section X, pp. 424-425.)

30. "A Free and Responsible Press," p. 97.

31. H. Gans, *Democracy and the News*, pp. 155-156 (note 32).

32. In his report to the Bollinger Task Force, Nicholas Lemann proposed a short, intensive skills-based course in the summer preceding the academic year.

33. Schell, "Some Ruminations on Journalism Schools as Columbia Turns," www.journalism.nyu.edu/pubzone/debate/forum.1.essay.schell.html.

34. Perhaps the Carnegie-Knight Journalism Initiative, a 3-year, $6 million program begun in 2005 by the Carnegie Corporation of New York and the John S. and James L. Knight Foundation, can help to move journalism education in this general direction. The Initiative, a joint-venture with the Joan Shorenstein Barone Center at Harvard and several leading journalism schools, is intended to "improve subject-matter education for journalists," develop investigative reporting projects, promote research, and encourage curricular enrichment and team-teaching between journalism schools and host universities. In addition to such initiatives, a Hutchins-type commission (but more diverse) should study journalism education in America, including not only journalists and journalism educators but leaders in other fields with no stake in the outcome. It is time to invite the public and the academy into the conversation about journalism education.

8

Clean News

Journalistic Excellence and Independence

> Such truth, as opposeth no man's profit, nor pleasure,
> is to all men welcome.
>
> **— Thomas Hobbes, "The Leviathan"**
> **(Review and Conclusion)**

I. No Strings Attached: the Value of Independence

Benjamin Franklin claimed in his *Autobiography* to have performed an experiment that few publishers would dare today. He slept on the floor and ate bread and water. "Finding I can live in this manner," he wrote, "I have formed a determination never to prostitute my press to the purposes of corruption and abuse ..." Independent journalism began in America with printers such as Franklin. Blogging and new media, with their ease of entry, and ease of access for the computer literate, hearken back to that tradition; but like the colonial printers, bloggers are not always rich repositories of factual information or original reporting.[1]

Drawing on earlier arguments, this chapter will suggest that independence of the kind Franklin proclaimed is conducive to journalistic excellence, and thus an important journalistic and democratic value. Such independence, defined as the absence of external influence or bias, is a virtue both in what we loosely identify as journalism's mainstream and in partisan discourse.

Strictly speaking, independence is neither a necessary nor a sufficient condition of journalistic excellence. The connection between independence and excellence is not automatic, but neither is it accidental. It is rather dispositional, like the connection between diet or exercise and health; it prevails much of the time. The world being a perverse and contradictory place, excellence sometimes commingles with profit, although seldom, if ever, with propaganda.

Independence differs from the other rubrics of excellence that we have identified in two closely related ways. First, it is not a form or component of excellence per se, or an end in itself, but rather an enabling condition, instrumental to those other forms of excellence: accuracy and truth, context and explanation, relevance and vigilance. Second, it pertains to journalistic institutions and to the overall political economy of the media, as well as to individual practitioners or institutions.

The value of independence is quite basic, rooted in the dual nature of most communication. Messages are normally received and recognized as if literally intended to inform. But the messenger's actual motives may be different or mixed: either to inform or to manipulate, or some combination of the two. Information is generally more valuable to the recipient when intended solely to inform, rather than to induce one to do, believe, or buy something. No rational person would choose to be swayed or deceived.

Able journalists function within compromised regimes, mostly in commercial journalism, as a matter of practical necessity. They are not all tainted by the pursuit of ratings or circulation, or by the government's propaganda interests; but such conditions limit what they can cover and how they can cover it. Journalism today is rife with conflicts between quality and profit. The very need for "firewalls" between business and editorial functions is evidence of this; recent history shows that such firewalls, where they exist, are often permeable.

As a democratic value, independence is, like freedom or excellence, formal and foundational: a basis on which further meaning may be built. It is in fact a kind of freedom: freedom from external influence or pressure. And like freedom in general, journalistic independence is always relative to some actual or possible threat. Such threats might include government censorship or cooptation; political parties, lobbies, or other ideological influences; or economic, cultural, or religious interests. (Explicitly political, religious, or other, media need make no excuses so long as they are transparent about their institutional biases and do not deceive audiences.)

Like freedom or excellence, independence is seldom a simple matter. Journalists, especially at the local level, need to be close to and independent of their communities, and that is a seeming contradiction. They must work professionally alongside colleagues and yet be independent of them, and that too creates conflict. We are talking about human beings and complex relationships here, not pipe-fitting. But if absolute independence, like perfect democracy, is a chimera, that is no reason to abandon the ideal. If independence meant having no motives or interests whatsoever, it would be a poor recipe for any kind of civic enterprise.

Here again, education provides a useful analogy. We do not educate young people simply to ensure their prosperity (although one important function of education is to promote individual economic productivity and self-sufficiency, which have civic as well as personal and societal value). Nor do we educate people to become partisans of the left, center, or right, although considered political commitments are all but essential to citizenship. We educate people, rather, to help them be self-reliant, self-actualizing, conscientious, and committed citizens, capable of leading full political, economic, cultural, social, civic, and spiritual lives. And that is how we should inform people as well. Independence, among other things, is what education and journalism are for.

There are two common ways in which factual information may be compromised (either distorted or suppressed): by subordination to economic interests (commercial bias), and by subordination to political interests (ideological bias). We discussed some aspects of ideological bias in Chapter 6; here, we will concentrate more on independence of the economic kind.[2]

Information supplied or sponsored by governments, parties, corporations, etc., does not always or necessarily undermine public awareness and understanding of events. Solid journalism may emanate from commercial or political enterprises despite mixed motives. (Useful and credible public information seldom comes from the upper reaches of power; a better source is the U.S. Government Printing Office.) But to the extent that information is insulated from profit or propaganda — the less it has to buck a (hidden or overt) financial or ideological riptide — the more credible and valuable it is to citizens, and the less likely to mislead.

Political and economic interests intertwine in various ways, sometimes inscrutably. Other things being equal, economic independence is an unalloyed good, and compromised messages — paid for by interested parties gaming the democratic system for their profit — are at best tolerable forms of propaganda, integral to the market, for example, as ways of burnishing a brand or stimulating demand. On the other hand, politically inflected messages, in the context of opinion or debate, are integral to democracy. Political bias is often a matter of individual opinion; economic bias is more often institutional or systemic.

Economic ownership interests tend to skew information politically to the right, whereas political bias may skew in any direction. Political values, moreover, reflect moral rather than monetary differences; they do not have the same material effect on the democratic system as dollars. Economic influence, in other words, is not just a bias but also a concrete form of power. Money, unlike an opinion, is convertible into something else. And it is often harder to detect ideological influence than to "follow the money." The power of money is seldom subtle.

Ideology differs from economic conflict in a deeper sense as well, because it gives political expression to such economic differences. In theory at least, democracy is a marketplace of ideas, based on a presumption of political equality, and not a marketplace of material values (there is another marketplace for those). That is why we cannot (overtly) buy and sell votes, political offices, or rights to citizenship. Political values shape the passage of laws, the execution of policy, the election and appointment of officials, and the overall character of the social contract, including the distribution of wealth.

To be sure, many (if not most) political values pertain to economic equality or inequality, but the debates about them, and the marketplace in which those debates occur, are fundamentally political. In a democracy, law (and politics, which determines what laws are passed and who passes them) controls money: "democracy must govern capitalism, not the other way around."³ In this sense, too, independence of information from economic interests is more important than political independence.

2.   Markets and Media

In a perfect world, journalism would be the exclusive purview of angels with no political or financial axes to grind. We are not quite there. But to say that there is a fundamental contradiction between capitalist media and democracy begs some questions. Practically speaking, capitalism and democracy are manifestly compatible, if perhaps not in their respective ideal forms. Both are elastic concepts, conceptually and in reality. Nowhere are they rigid, static, or absolute, except on occasion in the human mind.

Capitalism has also thrived in nondemocratic environments; but while democracy may coexist (in a more limited form) with laissez-faire capitalism, it thrives in more egalitarian societies, where higher levels of economic equality contribute to democratic political equality. In these societies, democracy strikes a different balance with capitalism's inherent tendency towards inequality. It is part of the genius of each system to adapt to the other, and one of democracy's basic functions is to adjust this balance over time.

The contradiction that concerns us is not the manageable, perhaps even necessary, one between capitalism and democracy. It is rather that of journalism trying to serve both masters: to provide the news that democratic citizens need, within a commercial context. As the Polish journalist Adam Michnik has observed, "[I]t is between the Scylla of the business plan and the Charybdis of the mission that we journalists have to swim."⁴ Many others have echoed the point; "The news, at best," writes Thomas Patterson, "is a workable compromise between the economic need of news organizations to attract and hold their audiences and the polity's need for a public forum."⁵

In truth, the whole business of making money from journalism is at least latently in conflict with its democratic role. Journalism can serve both masters, the mission and the business plan, but it cannot serve both faithfully and well. Commercial production of news has been the dominant paradigm for journalism virtually since its beginnings; Benjamin Franklin and his fellow colonial printers were not civic volunteers. The problem lies with the notion that journalistic excellence — journalism that promotes democracy through devotion to truth, context, and vigilance — is best served by that paradigm.

In any democratic society, some things are left to the market, some to the public sector, and some are subject to continual renegotiation. The recalibration of the public and private spheres is what democracy is all about. We do not allow private interests to own our roads, parks, public libraries or schools, or control the water supply. Nor do we let them run our justice system (despite recent ventures in privatizing corrections), interpret the Constitution, or oversee elections. We do not allow private institutions to negotiate on our behalf with foreign governments, raise armies or police forces, or collect our taxes. Nor are most schools (except for some vocational institutes) run for profit. Yet we allow corporations to create and distribute nearly all public information.

It might be argued that only commercial enterprises have the wherewithal to provide quality journalism. Doubtless in some instances that is the case; having more resources for reporting is usually better than having fewer. Yet wider claims for commercial journalism are undercut by its dismal recent history: widespread cost-cutting, including layoffs and overseas bureau-closings; indifference to localities and minorities; the increasing prostitution of journalistic values to entertainment and business values; stockholders' demands for greater profit margins from already-profitable media companies; and the detrimental impact of conglomeration on the quality and diversity of news (including the virtual disappearance of documentary journalism from television).[6]

Little if any of this is due to the poor performance of journalists or to a diminution of the available talent pool; nor is it because media corporations are unprofitable. (Average operating margins for newspapers in 2005 were 19.3 percent, twice the average among Fortune 500 companies.[7]) Rather, the decay is due to the commercial context of the news, and to decades of media concentration since the Hutchins Commission first warned of the dangers of commercialism and concentration sixty years ago. Newspapers that were run by conscientious families have been taken over by giant corporations and fund managers. Most media corporations care less about journalistic excellence than about rewarding their stockholders.

Media executives might reply that they are giving people what they want, and who can argue with that? Except for two things: first, desires are not given or immutable; and second, satisfying them does not necessarily get the work of democracy done. Our wants are stimulated, manipulated, even created, by advertising and popular culture (which increasingly merge with and debase the news). Giving us what we want is not so simple or innocent as it appears, even if we are entitled to it. Gratifying audiences does not sustain democracy, but often degrades it by inhibiting civic knowledge and engagement. The "wants" of a majority (or for that matter, a lucrative minority) may be incompatible with the civic needs of the public as a whole. So there is nothing wrong with commercial news, if we recognize it for what it is: a compromise with journalistic excellence and democratic ideals.

As a way of satisfying individual wants through transactions, the market is not an accidental process. It is what naturally emerges as a means of exchange and distribution in the absence of overseeing institutions, such as tribes, communes, governments, totalitarian parties, or bureaucracies. It is also in many respects a fair and efficient process, at least for some participants (and assuming perfect equality among the marketers). The market meets some of our most critical needs — for example, for food, clothing and shelter. We do not, in most cases, rely on government or other institutions for our survival; but if the market somehow failed to make food available, other means would be sought to avoid starvation.

If we can rely on the market for something as important as food, why not also for something like news? First, because the analogy rests on a false premise. The market is hardly a perfect mechanism for distributing food; there are still hungry and malnourished people. Second, while food is obviously more important than news, or even democracy, the need for news is not uniform, universal to humanity, or critical for survival. Whereas individually we need food to survive, the need for news relates to the common project of democracy, in which we have a nominally equal interest and say. To consign the news to the marketplace is to commercialize democracy itself.[8]

It is arguable whether everybody needs access to food of the same amount or quality; it is not necessary for survival, although eating better food may contribute to health and longevity. (If you really want health above all else, you might want to abjure the market entirely and consider growing your own food, or joining a co-op.) Whether some should eat better than others is a quintessentially moral and political question. But how to maximize the quality and availability of information — whether in schools, libraries, newspapers, on the air or on the Web — is a question about democracy itself and what it cedes to the market.

Food, moreover, is a finite resource which cannot be shared, whereas knowledge is mostly unlimited and divisible, at least once it has been created. Education is limited in terms of the relatively fixed number of great schools, teachers, libraries, etc.; but it is always possible for more people to read or learn.[9] Commerce largely dictates what foods are available to us; and, with very different implications, commerce also largely dictates what stories are covered, what views are heard, what ideas are entertained, and what frameworks are used.

3.   Clean News and the Independent Sector

An imperfect, but in many ways singularly successful, solution to conflicts between the public interest and the private has been the nonprofit sector, financed by both the public and private sectors but nominally independent of both. The love child of democracy and capitalism, the nonprofit sector historically has played two closely related roles: addressing human and community needs unmet by the other two sectors; and serving as a laboratory for experiments in the public interest. For several reasons, nonprofit enterprise is a natural alternative to the contradiction that is commercial journalism. The third sector can seek to maximize independence from both the state and capital, without threatening either. It does not need to be invented or require a revolution; and the other sectors have failed or are ineligible to do the job.

A larger nonprofit sector is, in fact, precisely what the Hutchins Commission — hardly a radical group — recommended for the American press. The report stated at the outset, in a rare moment of concision, that:

To demand that [the press] be free from pressures which might warp its utterance would be to demand that society should be empty of contending forces and beliefs. But persisting and distorting pressures — financial, popular, clerical, institutional — must be known and counterbalanced. The press must, if it is to be wholly free, know and overcome any biases incident to its own economic position, its concentration, and its pyramidal organization.[10]

The concluding section of *A Free and Responsible Press*, subtitled "What Can Be Done by the Public," is more explicit:

We recommend that nonprofit institutions help supply the variety, quantity, and quality of press service required by the American people ... the agencies of mass communication have a responsibility to the public like that of educational institutions ... [and] educational institutions have a responsibility to the public to use the instruments employed by the agencies of mass communications.[11]

Albion Ross, writing in the Center Magazine some twenty years later, argued similarly:

It is absurd to have the reporting of public affairs as a byproduct of the advertising industry. [It] is as vital to our society as is higher education. No one would think of transforming our colleges into advertising vehicles ... Are we so stultified and uninventive that the only press alternative we can imagine is government as publisher and broadcaster of public affairs? Are not the publicly tax-supported broadcasting systems in other democratic countries instructive? Is the example of our own publicly supported universities of no relevance?[12]

More recently, Gilbert Cranberg and others observed that the democratic functions of journalism "require the press to be free and independent of government, but they may require a measure of freedom from private markets, too, insofar as the private markets do not always place value ... on the oftentimes controversial, unsettling, and unwelcome gaze of the press's eye.[13]

It would be foolish to suppose that all journalism could, or should, be wholly independent of both the state and the market. The very definition of journalism is too vague for such rigidity. A thousand flowers should bloom — but not all within the same garden. The aim is not an exclusively noncommercial media system but rather what Robert W. McChesney calls "a more diverse and competitive commercial system with a significant nonprofit and noncommercial sector."[14]

"Clean news" — news that is not influenced by profit, ideology, faith, or any other special or vested interest — is no panacea.[15] But as a more independent journalistic model, it would promote excellence and enrich democratic discourse. We cannot expect all of our news to be perfectly pure and free of bias; what we need is enough independent reporting to constitute a viable alternative to commercial news. Nor do we expect our colleges and universities, as laboratories of democracy, to be wholly free from political ideas or influences. Just as we aim for tolerance and independence in education, we should do the same in journalism, which continues and extends the democratic dialogue begun within the academy.

Expansions of the public media sphere will not come from public agencies or private corporations, or from legislation. They must be created by citizens, as are most institutions in the independent sector. No simple lever exists for promoting clean news, nor can it be reduced to a single form or medium. Various strategies and models, including universities (which are already devoted to knowledge, democratic dialogue, and independence), community-based organizations, municipal- and employee-ownership, and foundations and private endowments, can contribute to the sea change in the culture of news that is now under way in America, and turn the commercial tide.[16]

Philanthropic endowments have a long and successful history of compensating for the shortcomings of the state and the market in other areas of public interest. Far-sighted individuals or foundations could broaden that base of nonprofit enterprise to include independent media. In fact, such calls for private media endowments go back a century or more. "It has been said," wrote an anonymous "independent journalist" in 1909, "that only generous endowment could 'emancipate' a great newspaper and enable it to be true to its highest ideals — to be honest in all things, to tell the truth boldly, to eschew sensationalism and vulgarity. And wealthy philanthropists have been urged to establish an 'exemplary,' a model newspaper, just as model libraries, model tenements, model orchestras are established by endowment."[17]

In the same era, Ferdinand Hansen advocated the establishment of a $1 billion fund to support independent newspapers;[18] and Edward Alsworth Ross, in a 1910 article for the *Atlantic Monthly,* envisioned "financially independent newspapers, the gift of public-spirited men of wealth." Such newspapers, he argued, free of commercial constraints and with community leaders serving on their governing boards, would have a salutary and "corrective" effect on the commercial press:

> Just as the moment came when it was seen that private schools, loan libraries, commercial parks, baths, gymnasia, athletic grounds, and playgrounds would not answer, so the moment is here for recognizing that the commercial news-medium does not adequately meet the needs of democratic citizenship. Endowment is necessary, and, since we are not yet wise enough to run a public-owned daily newspaper, the funds must come from private sources.[19]

Other voices, before and since Hutchins, have echoed these early calls for endowments or public funds for independent media. In 1922, David Sarnoff proposed a public service broadcasting organization, to be financed by a fee of two percent of gross revenues of the major networks; Walter Lippmann subsequently proposed using spectrum fees for the use of the airwaves, to fund a public news enterprise. (The BBC, funded by an annual tax on TV sets, is the world's largest journalism organization and one of the best, with 6,000 employees and a budget of about $6 billion.) In the 1970s, the sociologist and media theorist Herbert J. Gans proposed a national endowment for news.[20]

The endowment concept has limitations; it is contingent on the eleemosynary whims of billionaires or their foundations; and while not undemocratic, it is extra-democratic (as are commercial media and other nonprofit ventures), rather than a direct reflection of the public will. In the long run, some form of public subsidy and/or tax on advertising profits might be preferable. But news endowments would also offer several advantages: they do not have to wait for the long run; they can afford to be experimental, and to fail, as public media initiatives cannot; they can pioneer new paths without depending on cultural shifts or democratic majorities to support them; and they can self-perpetuate, like endowments for museums, hospitals, libraries, colleges, and other institutions, making no claims on public resources. The complementary solution is obvious, and in fact is in process: citizens need to create their own independent news organizations, professional and otherwise.

However structured, clean news — like clean elections — would be a boon to democracy and to free and diverse speech. Other countries have long since discovered that commercialism and state propaganda are not the only alternatives. We do not rely on corporations to run our education system; on the contrary, independent, nonprofit education is one of the pillars of American democracy. So we return to Albion Ross's question: why should journalism, as a crucial source of public education, be any different?

A consortium of major foundations, universities, and individual benefactors could easily create a significant nonprofit, multimedia journalistic enterprise. In the meantime, Joan Kroc's bequest in 2003 of some $230 million of her McDonald's fortune to National Public Radio is a promising investment in independent media. And one of the nation's best newspapers, the *St. Petersburg Times*, is owned by the Poynter Institute for Media Studies, a nonprofit educational institution.[21]

The Internet has already provided a significant venue for independent journalism, including some produced within academic settings.[22] Community-based, open-source journalism and alternative journalism are providing important conduits of information that is neither in the commercial mainstream nor mere rumor or invective. But there is also a need for professional journalism that challenges the commercial monopoly of the mainstream. Of course, the terms *professional* and *mainstream* are relative and only loosely definable. There will always be gradations of quality, neutrality, independence, and professionalism. But it is possible to pursue all of these values at once. There is daylight between the idea of a commercial mainstream, appealing to the lowest common denominator, and alternatives that are either implacably political or nonprofessional.

4.   The Wayward Press

The Hutchins Report concluded with thirteen recommendations. Some of them were rather vague; for example, it urged that the government "facilitate new ventures in the communications industry, that it foster the introduction of new techniques …" and urged the use of antitrust laws to prevent undue concentration. It invited the government to "employ media of its own" to inform the public of its policies, a nostrum that may now sound quaint or naïve. Yet, overall, the ideas are sound and, if anything, even more compelling in the current media landscape than in their own time.

The report urged the press to accept responsibility for being common carriers; "They must therefore be hospitable to ideas and attitudes different from their own, and they must present them to the public as meriting its attention." The press was further admonished to "assume the responsibility of financing new, experimental activities in the field" along with nonprofit institutions. The report recommended that "members of the press engage in vigorous mutual criticism." And it urged the public to act on its own to create nonprofit media.

Finally, the commission recommended the creation of "academic-professional centers of advanced study, research, and publication in the field of communications [and] that existing schools of journalism exploit the total resources of their universities to the end that their students may obtain the broadest and most liberal training." And it urged "the establishment of a new and independent agency to appraise and report annually upon the performance of the press." The overall theme is a clear echo of Joseph Pulitzer's vision for journalism education: not just noncommercial, but anticommercial.

In the Hutchins tradition, an array of specific reforms to foster independent journalism, locally and nationally, have been proposed by various media critics, and in particular by McChesney.[23] These include deconcentration of the commercial media through more vigorous antitrust action and caps on ownership, and greater support (as well as more independence) for public broadcasting. Reformers also urge the awarding of licenses for low-power FM radio stations to nonprofit organizations, free airtime for political candidates, and more challenges to commercial FCC licenses.

We could add to the list anything that encourages noncommercial media, local media, media diversity: the very things that are threatened (if that is not too mild a word) by the existing commercial-conglomerate system. Journalism schools, as suggested earlier, should become handmaidens of excellence by forming a natural bridge between the world of reporting and the world of research and teaching. They should be instrumental in hosting local and regional journalism reviews, as well as town hall meetings for interchange between the public and the news media. It is time to reform not just journalism education but the very identity and public image of journalism, and rebrand it as a public enterprise.

Several legislative measures deserve consideration. We need legislation preventing the government from lying to us at our own expense, either directly or by using corrupt journalists.[24] The Bush Administration in its first term spent a record $254 million on such propaganda, much of it fake news designed to look real, touting the Administration's policies. (This misuse of government is the very specter that conservatives invoke to prevent the government from playing even an indirect role within the ecology of public discourse.) In addition, we need to protect government whistle-blowers. Public employees — from agency bureaucrats to generals — must be able to disseminate information in the public interest free of government censorship or retribution.

For citizens, supporting tax write-offs for nonprofit journalism would be a good place to begin. But if we want better journalism, we must also support better education standards and better-paid teachers; that is where the demand for journalistic excellence originates. Do we really want a more robust democracy? If so, then our children must be more knowledgeable, curious, critical, engaged, and media literate than we are — not just better at text messaging.

Many of us think of "the media" as an alien and vaguely hostile force. That may be one reason why so many refer to it, incorrectly, in the singular. We would do better to be more micro-critical of specific institutions, journalists, or stories, and less macro-critical of the media as a whole, when in fact the media are our democratic surrogate. Of course schools should put more emphasis on media literacy as a set of essential skills for citizenship — including knowing how to produce, consume, and interpret news media. But just as important is familiarity with the news. As David T. Z. Mindich has sensibly suggested, either the SAT I or the optional SAT II (or both) should include a current events section.[25]

We also need to ask ourselves some new questions. What if some news outlets were owned and operated by journalism schools or universities, or community organizations? What if journalism education were considered a public-interest field, like education or social work? What if we looked upon commercial news as an oddity, like commercial schools? What if we saw the Internet as a possible venue for noncommercial news, rather than an instant source of everything unproven, narcissistic, or unprofessional?

Such proposals for journalistic reconstruction are no more radical than the fundamental changes envisioned, and seen, in previous eras of American journalism since the emergence of the penny press in the 1830s. The question is not whether change is coming but of what kind; not whether we want to live in a democracy but how democratic we want it to be.

5. Democratic Spheres

Democracy is not just a formal system of government; it is an evolving social organism. Forms and levels of democratic order, primarily in terms of political accountability and political equality, are relative to the evolutionary stages of democracy's organic components: law, culture, knowledge, technology, economic production. Democracies do not simply unfold on their own, but coevolve along with these systemic parts. And the quality of journalism, as this book has argued, is a coefficient of democracy: a key determinant of its meaning and scope.

At some indeterminate point in this evolutionary process, education and journalism come to be recognized as core democratic values for informed political (as well as cultural and economic) citizenship. In the United States, a strong vein of libertarian antistatism has in some ways retarded that evolution. At the same time, traditions of localism and federalism have advanced it, for example, through public education, public libraries, advocacy organizations, and nonprofit institutions in general, relatively free of both state and commercial influence; and by mediating between government, the private sector, and public needs. (We have also had public support of the media since the early days of the Republic through postal subsidies.)

The question now is how to foster an independent media sector, promoting democratic evolution in keeping with the American genius for nonprofit public enterprise. Important forms of independent media are emerging spontaneously, especially on to the Internet. Such media, free of the tyranny of the market, could hasten this evolution toward a more vital and unified continuum of learning and a more robust democracy. But to get there, we need to finally explode the uncritical dualistic assumption that the market and state propaganda are the only possible sources of information. And until there are higher levels of computer literacy and media literacy, the Internet cannot be considered a panacea for informed citizenship. Neither is the imaginative use of private wealth a panacea; but it can usefully fund experiments and sow the seeds of change.

Ultimately, it is public consciousness of what a democracy is, and what it requires and promises, that determines the pace and course of change. Paradoxically, such consciousness is both a cause and a result of education and journalism. We are evolving, slowly and uncertainly, toward a conception of democracy that embraces robust citizenship: citizens with multiple (political, media, computer, economic, and cultural) literacies. Journalism is integral to that mix.

Democratic journalism, like politics, must always be in a state of crisis: a state of conflict, debate, and change. It is charged with meaning and value, yet susceptible to all of the flaws, distortions, and biases endemic to human communication. As we have noted, nothing (other than popular demand) assures that we have any journalism at all; yet democracies are contingent on its existence and conditioned by its quality. That is the main paradox described in this book — the peculiar dependence of democracies on the quality of available information, and people's ability to process it and act on it — and there is no simple resolution.

Democratic governments cannot have unlimited power over the information sphere; but leaving that sphere entirely to market forces is likewise inimical to democracy. It has led to monopoly concentration, the dampening or suppression of minority voices, the narrowing of the range of acceptable opinion and taste, limits on the diversity of coverage and the coverage of diversity, unequal access, isolation of smaller groups and communities from journalistic attention, and above all, the pervasive degradation of news by entertainment values.

Of course the news must be relevant to our lives as citizens, producers and consumers, and members of overlapping communities. But its aim is not to palliate or entertain us. We would do better to paraphrase John F. Kennedy: *Ask not what the news can do for you. Ask what you can do with the news.*

Particular obstacles to excellence, commercial or otherwise, can be identified and overcome. But the quality of news is only one side of the problem: the supply side. The demand side is equally if not more elusive: improving the quality of education so that informed and engaged citizens will demand excellence in journalism, and use it once they get it. Without stimulating that demand, there is not much point worrying about the supply. The situation is indeed circular, because education and journalism interconnect with one another, and with economic resources, cultural conditions, and the gears and levers of democracy.

Hence, the quest for journalistic excellence naturally raises parallel questions about excellence in education: what is it, how do we identify and measure and maximize it? How exactly is journalism subsidiary to it? Recognizing differences of human ability, ambition, and interest, how do we improve the media and avoid the scourges of commercialism and elitism? But we are not just talking in circles. Rather, democracy itself is about interlocking circles: politics, law and money, news and entertainment, citizens and consumers, the culture and technologies that frame those systems, and the ideals that give them moral purpose. These spheres form a complex ecology; to grasp the complexity and importance of journalistic excellence within that ecology is to see the big picture.

Endnotes

1. Blogging is a paradigm of radical independence, but it is not conventional journalism and seldom involves original reporting. Like the Lone Ranger, bloggers may function effectively, but they lack the institutional resources

and filters — the talent pools, editorial review, investigatory resources, access to news sources and sites, professionalism, defined public mission, etc. — of news organizations. Blogging can produce journalism, and it can provide an important fact-checking function, correcting journalistic inaccuracies. But it can also serve as an echo-chamber for rumor and polemic.

2. As noted earlier, various other types of bias, such as sponsorship by interest groups, religious institutions, labor unions, political parties, etc., tend to be marginal to the mainstream and targeted at narrower audiences, and represent legitimate (and important) forms of advocacy.

3. K.K. Campbell, "Marketing Public Discourse," *The Hedgehog Review* (Fall 2004): p. 54.

4. Michnik, in A. Michnik and J. Rosen, "The Media and Democracy: A Dialogue," *Journal of Democracy* 8:4 (Oct. 1997): p. 88.

5. Patterson, T.E., "The United States: News in a Free-Market Society," in R. Gunther and A. Mughan, eds., *Democracy and the Media: A Comparative Perspective*, p. 264.

6. Numerous books have catalogued the decline of journalism, including James Fallows's *Breaking the News*, and Tom Fenton's *Bad News*.

7. See J.S. Carroll, "What Will Become of Newspapers?" p. 8.

8. Recall that democracy is primary; it is through the democratic process, for example, that we decide whether or how to offset the market as a distributor of food.

9. Even credentials such as educational degrees are arguably a limited resource, useful only for distinguishing levels of education among individuals in order to confer comparative advantage; if everyone had Ph.D.'s, there would be no reason for Ph.D.'s to exist. But the same is not true of the overall value of education.

10. The Hutchins Commission, "A Free and Responsible Press"; p. 18.

11. Ibid., p. 97.

12. A. Ross, 1966; reprinted in *The Center Magazine*, March/April 1987, p. 34.

13. G. Cranberg et al., *Taking Stock: Journalism and the Publicly Traded Company*. Ames, IA: Iowa State U. Press, 2001; p. 138.

14. McChesney, "The U.S. Left and Media Politics," Monthly Review Vol. 50(9) insert (February 1999): p. 40.

15. The term "special interest," however, should be used with care, as its common usage embraces both public (nonprofit) interest groups and groups representing commercial interests. Proponents of the latter have very effectively exploited this ambiguity to their advantage.

16. In the mainstream media, there are several nonprofit newspapers, including the *Christian Science Monitor* and the *St. Petersburg Times*, which is owned by the nonprofit Poynter Institute, and the Associated Press is a nonprofit cooperative of member news organizations.

17. An Independent Journalist, "Is an Honest and Sane Newspaper Possible?" *The American Journal of Sociology*, 15:3 (Nov. 1909): p. 322.

18. Hansen: see *H. Hardt, Social Theories of the Press*, pp. 153 ff.; Hardt cites the German sociologist Ferdinand Tönnies [Kritik der öffentlichen Meinung (Berlin, 1922), p. 574] as another early proponent of independent media.

19. Edward Alsworth Ross, "The Suppression of Important News," *Atlantic Monthly* (March, 1910): p. 310.

20. H.J. Gans, "Federal Funding For News Coverage," *The New York Times* (April 30, 1979): A-17.

21. Another interesting experiment, if market and cultural biases do not defeat it, Al Jezeera English, inaugurated in 2006 with funding from the Qatar royal family.

22. "War News Radio," organized by students at Swarthmore College to cover the war in Iraq, is an example. The author has supported War News Radio.

23. For one of the most extensive road maps of media reform, see Robert W. McChesney's "Making Media Democratic," *The Boston Review*, Summer 1998; online at www.bostonreview.net/BR23.3/mcchesney.html, or his numerous books, including *Our Media Not Theirs*, co-authored by John Nichols. McChesney calls for both expanded nonprofit media (with tax-incentivized public contributions) and a vastly increased subsidy for public media, to put the U.S. on a par with other democracies such as Britain and Japan. These would not only provide higher-quality and more diverse alternatives to commercial media, but might well spur improvement in some of those media as well.

24. Perhaps the public interest in truth should not override the First Amendment right of journalism organizations to lie, for example, by using corporate or political VNR's (video news releases) without disclosing their true nature.

25. "There's no reason," writes Mindich, "why print and broadcast news shouldn't be a bigger part of the school curriculum, or why there shouldn't be a short civics/current affairs section on the SAT for college-bound students, or why all high school seniors shouldn't have to take a nonbinding version of the civics test given to immigrants who want to become U.S. citizens. And why shouldn't broadcasters be required to produce a certain amount of children's news programming in return for their access to the

public airwaves? These are only the most obvious possibilities." (*Just the Facts: How 'Objectivity' Came to Define American Journalism*. NY: New York University Press, 1998): p. 53.

Bibliography

Adam, G.S., *Notes towards a Definition of Journalism,* The Poynter Institute for Media Studies, St. Petersburg, FL, 1993.

Journalism and the university: Reporters, writers and critics, in *The Idea of the University: 1789–1989,* Jaeger, K., Ed., Conference Publication No. 3. Institute for Advanced Study, University of King's College, Halifax, NS, 1990.

Adhikari, G., From the press to the media, *Journal of Democracy,* 11 (1), 56–63, 2000.

Akst, D.Nonprofit journalism: Removing the pressure of the bottom line, *The Carnegie Reporter,* 3 (3), 2005. See also: C. Connell et al., "Journalism's Crisis of Confidence."

Alexander, J.C., The mass news media in systemic, historical, and comparative perspective, in *Mass Media and Social Change,* Katz, E. and Szecskö, T., Eds., Sage, Beverly Hills, 1981.

Allan, S., *News Culture,* Open University Press, Philadelphia, 1999.

Alterman, E., *Sound and Fury: The Making of the Punditocracy,* Cornell University Press, Ithaca, 1999.

Anderson, R.D., Jr., The place of the media in popular democracy, *Critical Review,* 12 (4), 481–500, 1998.

Anon. (An Independent Journalist), Is an honest and sane newspaper possible? *American Journal of Sociology,* 15 (3), 321–334. 1909.

Arendt, H., Truth and politics, *Between Past and Future: Eight Exercises in Political Thought,* (Viking, New York, 1961); Penguin Books, 1977.

Ashmore, H. *Unseasonable Truths: The Life of Robert Maynard Hutchins,* Little, Brown and Co., Boston, 1989.

Auletta, K., Annals of communication: Fault line, *The New Yorker,* Oct. 10, 2005, p. 51–61.

_____. Big Bird flies right: How Republicans learned to love PBS, *The New Yorker,* June 7, 2004, pp. 42–48.

Baggini, J. *Making Sense: Philosophy behind the Headlines,* Oxford University Press, 2002.

Barnhurst, K.G. and Nerone, J., *The Form of News: A History,* The Guilford Press, New York, 2001.

Barzun, J., Is democratic theory for export? *Ethics and International Affairs,* 1, 53–71, 1987.

Bates, S., Realigning journalism with democracy: The Hutchins Commission, its times, and ours, The Annenberg Washington Program in Communications Policy Studies of Northwestern University, 1995; www.annenberg. nwu.edu/pubs/Hutchins/default.htm.

Blanchard, M.A., The Hutchins Commission, the press and the responsibility concept, *Journalism Monographs,* 49, 1–59, 1977.

Blitz, M. The media we deserve, *The Public Interest,* 159, 125–138, 2005.

Bourdieu, P., *On Television,* The New Press, New York, 1996.

Bowman, J. , All McKinneys now, *The New Criterion,* 24 (2), 61–65, 2005.

Brown, M. , Abandoning the news, *Carnegie Reporter,* Carnegie Corporation of New York, Spring, 2005. (See also: Connell, C., et al.). http://www.carnegie.org/reporter/10/news/index.html.

Campbell, K.K., Marketing public discourse, *The Hedgehog Review,* Fall, 39–54, 2004.

Carey, J.W., *Communication as Culture,* Routledge, New York, 1992.

_____. The Struggle against Forgetting, Columbia Graduate School of Journalism (Web site), 1995. www.jrn.columbia.edu/admissions/struggle/.

_____. The Mass media and democracy: Between the modern and the post-modern, *Journal of International Affairs,* 47 (1), 1–21, 1993.

_____. Foreword. Hardt, H., *Social Theories of the Press: Early German and American Perspectives,* Beverly Hills: Sage Publications, 1979.

Carey, J.W., et al., The press and public discourse, *The Center Magazine,* March–April, 4–32, 1987.

Carey, J(ohn), Ed., *The Faber Book of Reportage,* Faber and Faber Ltd., London, 1987.

Carroll, J.S., What Will Become of Newspapers? Joan Shorenstein Center on the Press, Politics and Public Policy, John F. Kennedy School of Government, Harvard University, 2006.

Chinni, D., Measuring the news media's effectiveness, *Nieman Reports,* Summer, 98–99, 2004.

Corner, J., Ideology: A note on conceptual salvage, *Media Culture and Society,* 23 (4), 525–533, 2001.

Cohen, E.D., Ed., *Philosophical Issues in Journalism,*and Oxford University Press, New York, 1992.

Cohen, J.L. and Arato, A., Civil society and political theory, in Blaug, R. and Schwartzmantel, J., Eds., *Democracy: A Reader,* Columbia University Press, New York, 2001.

Cohen, R., It's not news: What today's high school journalist is taught, *Harper's Magazine,* Feb. 2004, pp. 65–72.

Connell, C., et al., Journalism's Crisis of Confidence: A Challenge for the Next Generation: A Report of Carnegie Corporation of New York, 2006. http://www.carnegie.org/pdf/journalism_crisis/journ_crisis_full.pdf

Cranberg, G., Bezanson, R., and Soloski, J., *Taking Stock: Journalism and the Publicly Traded Company,* Iowa State University Press, Ames, IA, 2001.

Cunningham, B., Rethinking objectivity, *Columbia Journalism Review,* July–Aug., 24–32, 2003.

Dahl, R.A., *Democracy and Its Critics,* Yale University Press, New Haven, 1989.

———. *On Democracy,* Yale University Press, New Haven, 1998.

Darnton, R., Writing news and telling stories, *Daedalus,* 104, 175–194, 1975.

Dennis, E.E. and Snyder, R.W., Eds., *Media and Public Life,* Transaction Publishers, New Brunswick, NJ, 1997.

Dewey, J. , Public opinion (review), *The New Republic,* May 3, 1922.

———. *The Public and Its Problems,* Henry Holt, New York, 1927.

Dewey, J., et al., *The Philosopher of the Common Man: Essays in Honor of John Dewey to Celebrate His Eightieth Birthday,* Greenwood Press, New York, 1968.

Downie, L. and Kaiser, R.G., *The News about the News: American Journalism in Peril,* Random House/Vintage Books, New York, 2002.

Doyle, L. and Gitler, M., Brits vs. Yanks: Who does journalism right? *Columbia Journalism Review,* May–June, 44–49, 2004.

Dzuback, M.A., *Robert M. Hutchins: Portrait of an Educator,* University of Chicago Press, 1991.

Eastland, T., Starting over, *The Wilson Quarterly,* Spring, 40–47, 2005.

Eco, U., On the press, in *Five Moral Pieces,* McEwan, A., Trans., Harcourt, New York, 2001.

The Economist, More media, less news, Aug. 26, 2006, pp. 52–54.

The Economist, Who killed the newspaper? Aug. 26, 2006, pp. 9–10.

Ekström, M., Epistemologies of TV journalism: A theoretical framework, *Journalism,* 3 (3), 259–282, 2002.

Entman, R.M., *Democracy without Citizens: Media and the Decay of American Politics,* Oxford University Press, New York, 1989.

Epstein, E.J. *Between Fact and Fiction: The Problem of Journalism,* Vintage Books, New York, 1975.

Ettema, J. and Glasser, T., On the epistemology of investigative journalism, *Communication,* 8 (2), 183–206, 1985.

_____. Investigative Journalism and the moral order, *Critical Studies in Mass Communication,* 6, 1–20, 1989.

Fenton, T. *Bad News: The Decline of Reporting, the Business of News, and the Danger to Us All,* HarperCollins, New York, 2005.

Finnegan, L. *No Questions Asked: A Critical Look at News Coverage in the U.S. after the September 11, 2001 Attacks,* Praeger, Westport, CT, 2007.

Frankel, M., The facts of media life, *The New York Times,* Sept. 27, 1998, pp. 32–34.

The Nirvana news, *The New York Times Magazine,* July 9, 2000, pp. 16–18.

Fraser, N., To BBC or not to BBC: Independent journalism suffers an identity crisis, *Harper's Magazine,* May 2004, pp. 55–64.

Freedman, S.G., *Letters to a Young Journalist,* Basic Books, New York, 2006.

Friedman, J., Public opinion: Bringing the media back in, *Critical Review,* 15 (3–4), 239–260, 2003.

Gans, H.J., *Deciding What's News,* Pantheon, New York, 1979.

_____. Federal Funding for news coverage, *The New York Times,* April 30, 1979, p. A-17.

_____. *Democracy and the News,* Oxford University Press, 2003.

Gauthier, G., In defence of a supposedly outdated notion: The range of application of journalistic objectivity, *Canadian Journal of Communications,* 18 (4), 1993.

Gavin, T., The truth beyond facts: Journalism and literature, *The Georgia Review,* 45 (1), 39–51, 1991.

Gitlin, T., *Media Unlimited: How the Torrent of Images and Sounds Overwhelms Our Lives,* Metropolitan Books, New York, 2001.

_____. Deliberation in democracy, *The Hedgehog Review,* Fall, 7–13, 2004.

_____. *The Intellectuals and the Flag,* Columbia University Press, New York, 2006.

Gopnik, A., Read all about it, *The New Yorker,* Dec. 12, 1994, pp. 84–102.

_____. The end of the world: Crisis at France's most venerable paper, *The New Yorker,* Nov. 15, 2004, pp. 64–71.

Gorney, C., *The Business of News: A Challenge for Journalisms's Next Generation,* The Carnegie Corporation, New York, 2002.

Gramsci, A., Journalism, *Selections from Cultural Writings,* Forgacs, D. and Nowell-Smith, Eds., Harvard University Press, Cambridge, 1991.

Gunther, R. and Mughan, A., Eds., *Democracy and the Media: A Comparative Perspective,* Cambridge University Press, 2000.

Habermas, J., The public sphere, in *Rethinking Popular Culture,* Mukerji, C. and Schudson, M., Eds., University of California Press, Berkeley, 1991.

————. *The structural transformation of the public sphere: An inquiy into a category of bourgeois society.* Translated by Thomas Burger. Cambridge: MIT Press, 1991.

————. The public sphere: An encyclopedia article, *New German Critique,* 3, 49–55, 1974; also in *Democracy: A Reader,* Blaug, R. and Schwartzmantel, J., Eds., Columbia Univeresity Press, New York, 2001.

Hackett, R. and Zhao, Y., Journalistic objectivity and social change, *Peace Review,* 8 (1), 5–11, 1996.

————. *Sustaining Democracy? Journalism and the Politics of Objectivity,* Garamond, Toronto, 1998.

Hallin, D., and Mancini, P., *Comparing Media Systems: Three Models of Media and Politics,* Cambridge University Press, 2004.

Hallock, S.M. , *Editorial and Opinion: The Dwindling Marketplace of Ideas in Today's News,* Praeger, Westport, CT, 2007.

Hamill, P. , *News Is a Verb: Journalism at the End of the Twentieth Century*, Ballantine, New York, 1998.

Hamilton, J., Alternative media: Conceptual difficulties, critical possibilities, *Journal of Communication Inquiry,* 24 (4), 357–378, 2000.

Hardt, H., *Social Theories of the Press: Early German and American Perspectives,* Sage Publications, Beverly Hills, CA, 1979.

Hersey, J., The legend on the license, *Yale Review,* 75 (2), 289–314, 1986.

Hughes, D. , *The Hack's Tale: Hunting the Makers of the Media: Chaucer, Froissart, Boccaccio,* Bloomsbury Publishing, London, 2004.

Janeway, M. , *Republic of Denial: Press, Politics, and Public Life,* Yale University Press, New Haven, 1999.

Johnson, K.G., Epistemology and responsibility of the mass media, *ETC: A Review of General Semantics,* 61 (4), 663–675, 2004. Reprinted from: *General Semantics Bulletin.* nos. 41–43, 1977.

Johnson, T. J., Hayes, C.E., and Hayes, S.P. Eds., *Engaging the Public: How Government and the Media Can Reinvigorate American Democracy,* Rowman and Littlefield, Lanham, MD, 1998.

Jones, A., The inestimable value of family ownership, *Nieman Reports,* Fall, 63–64, 1999.

Kellner, D., *Media Spectacle and the Crisis of Democracy,* Paradigm Publishers, London, 2005.

Kenner, H., The politics of the plain style, in *Literary Journalism in the Twentieth Century,* Sims, N., Ed., : Oxford University Press, New York, 1990.

Kitty, A., Appeals to authority in journalism, *Critical Review,* 15 (3–4), 347–357, 2003.

Kovach, B. and Rosenstiel, T., *The Elements of Journalism: What Newspeople Should Know and the Public Should Expect,* Crown, New York, 2001.

Kramer, M., Breakable rules for literary journalism, in *Literary Journalism: A New Collection of the Best American Nonfiction,* Sims, N., Ed., Ballantine Books, New York, 1995.

Kunkel, T., Leaving readers behind: The age of corporate newspapering, (Pew Charitable Trusts) *American Journalism Review,* May, 2001. www.ajr.org/ article.asp?id=263

Lakoff, G. *Don't Think of an Elephant! Know Your Values and Frame the Debate,* Chelsea Green Publishing, White River Jct., VT, 2004.

Leigh, R., Ed., *A Free and Responsible Press: A General Report on Mass Communication: Newspapers, Radio, Motion Pictures, Magazines, and Books,* Commission on Freedom of the Press, University of Chicago Press, Chicago, 1947.

Lemann, N., Fear and favor, *The New Yorker,* Feb. 14 and 21, 168–176, 2005.

Amateur hour: Journalism without journalists, *The New Yorker,* Aug. 7 and 14, 44–49, 2006.

The Murrow doctrine, *The New Yorker,* Jan. 23 and 30, 38–43, 2006.

Leverette, M., Towards an ecology of understanding: Semiotics, medium theory, and the uses of meaning, *Image and Narrative,* Jan. 2003; www.imageand-narrative.be/mediumtheory/marcleverette.htm.

Lewis, A., What privileges for the press? (review) *The New York Review of Books,* 52, (12), 4–8, 2005.

Liebling, A.J., *The Wayward Pressman,* Doubleday and Co., Garden City, NY, 1947.

_____. Some reflections on the American press, *The Nation,* April 12, 1947, p. 427.

_____. *The Press,* Ballantine Books, New York, 1961.

Lyons, G., The media is the message: Notes on our decadent press, *Harper's Magazine,* Oct. 2003, pp. 77–82.

Mander, J., *Four Arguments for the Elimination of Television,* Quill, New York, 1978.

Maynard, N.H., The journalist as storyteller, *Gannett Center Journal,* Spring, 78–84, 1988.

McIntyre, J.S., Repositioning a landmark: The Hutchins Commission and freedom of the press, *Critical Studies in Mass Communication,* 4 (2), June,136–160, 1987.

Macpherson, C.B., *The Real World of Democracy,* Oxford University Press, 1966.

Massing, M., *Now They Tell Us: The American Press and Iraq,* New York Review Books, New York, 2004.

_____. The end of news? *The New York Review of Books,* Dec. 1, 2005, pp. 23–27.

_____. The press: The enemy within, *The New York Review of Books,* Dec. 15, 2005, pp. 36–44.

McChesney, R.W., *Corporate Media and the Threat to Democracy,* Seven Stories Press, New York, 1997.

_____. Making media democratic, *Boston Review,* Summer 1998; www.boston-review.net/BR23.3/mcchesney.html.

_____. The U.S. Left and Media Politics, *Monthly Review,* 50 (9 (Feb. 1999): 32–41.

_____. Journalism, democracy and class struggle, *Monthly Review,* 52 (6), 1–15, 2000.

_____. The problem of journalism, *Journalism Studies,* 4 (3) 299–330, 2003.

_____. *Rich Media, Poor Democracy,* University of Illinois Press, Chicago, 1999.

_____. *The Problem of the Media: U.S. Communication Politics in the 21ˢᵗ Century,* Monthly Review Press, New York, 2004.

McChesney, R.W. and Nichols, J., Up in flames: The public revolts against monopoly media, *The Nation,* Nov. 17, 2003, pp. 11–14.

McChesney, R.W. and Scott, B., Upton Sinclair and the contradictions of capitalist journalism, *Monthly Review,* 54 (1), 1–14, 2002.

Meijer, I.C., What is quality television news? *Journalism Studies,* 4 (1), 15–29, 2003.

Meilleur, M., John Dewey redux, *The Antioch Review,* 61 (1), 173–184, 2005.

Merrill, J., *Journalism Ethics: Philosophical Foundations for News Media,* St. Martin's Press, New York, 1997.

Meyer, P., Saving journalism: How to nurse the good stuff until it pays, *Columbia Journalism Review,* Nov.–Dec.,55–57, 2004.

Mindich, D.T.Z., *Just the Facts: How 'Objectivity' Came to Define American Journalism,* New York University Press, New York, 1998.

_____. The young and the restless, *The Wilson Quarterly,* Spring, 48–53, 2005.

Minogue, K., Journalism: Power without responsibility, *The New Criterion,* Feb., 4–13, 2005.

Moyers, B., *Moyers on America: A Journalist and His Times,* Anchor Books, New York, 2004.

Munson, E.S., and Warren, C.A., Eds., *James Carey: A Critical Reader,* University of Minnesota Press, Minneapolis, 1997.

Newman, J., *The Journalist in Plato's Cave,* Associated University Presses, Cranbury, NJ, 1989.

Nichols, C. McK., What would the public think? An experiment in deliberative democracy, *The Hedgehog Review,* Fall, 67–76, 2004.

Nichols, J., How to free the press, *The Nation,* April 17, 2006, pp. 5–6.

Norris, P., *A Virtuous Circle: Political Communications in Postindustrial Societies,* Cambridge University Press, 2000.

Park, R.E., News as a form of knowledge: A chapter in the sociology of knowledge, *American Journal of Sociology,* 45, 669–686, 1940.

Patterson, T.E., The United States: News in a free-market society, in *Democracy and the Media: A Comparative Perspective,* Gunther, R. and Mughan, A., Eds., Cambridge University Press, 2000.

Pennypacker, S.W., Sensational journalism and the remedy, *North American Review,* 190 (648) 587–593, 1909.

Pew Research Center for the People and the Press, *Striking the Balance: Audience Interests, Business Pressures and Journalists' Values,* The Center, Washington, DC, 1999.

Platon, S. and Deuze, M., Indymedia journalism: A radical way of making, selecting and sharing news? *Journalism,* 4 (3), 336–355, 2003.

Postman, N., *Amusing Ourselves to Death,* Viking Penguin, New York, 1985.

_____. *Conscientious Objections: Stirring Up Trouble about Language, Technology, and Education,* Alfred A. Knopf, New York, 1988.

Postman, N. and Powers, S., *How to Watch TV News,* Penguin Books, New York, 1992.

Powers, W., Seven steps to salvation, *The Wilson Quarterly,* Spring, 54–59, 2005.

Quindlen, A., Journalism 101: Human nature, *Newsweek,* Nov. 15, 1999, p. 104.

Raines, H., My times, *The Atlantic,* May, 49–81, 2004.

Randall, V., Ed., *Democratization and the Media,* Frank Cass, Portland, OR, 1998.

Rosen, J., Politics, vision, and the press: Toward a public agenda for journalism, in *The New News v. the Old News: The Press and Politics in the 1990s,* Rosen, J. and Taylor, P., Twentieth Century Fund, 1992.

_____. *What Are Journalists For?* Yale University Press, New Haven, 1999.

Ross, A., Public affairs journalism, *The Center Magazine,* March–April, 33–35, 1987.

Ross, E.A., The suppression of important news, *Atlantic Monthly,* March, 303–311, 1910.

Rowley, K.M. and Kurpius, D.D., There's a new gatekeeper in town: How statewide public affairs television creates potential for an altered media model, *Journalism and Mass Communication Quarterly,* 82 (1), 167–180, 2005.

Rucinski, D., The centrality of reciprocity to communication and democracy, *Critical Studies in Mass Communication,* 8 (2), 184–194, 1991.

Russell, C.E., The press and the public, *La Follete's Magazine,* June 4, 1910, p. 7.

Sanders, K., *Ethics and Journalism,* Sage Publications, Thousand Oaks, CA, 2003.

Schmuhl, R., Ed., *The Responsibilities of Journalism,* University of Notre Dame Press, 1984.

Schudson, M., *Discovering the News: A Social History of American Newspapers,* Basic Books, New York, 1978.

_____. *The Power of News,* Harvard University Press, Cambridge, 1995.

_____. Why conversation is not the soul of democracy, *Critical Studies in Mass Communication,* 14, 297–309, 1997.

_____. The objectivity norm in American journalism, *Journalism,* 2 (2), 149–170, 2001.

Sen, A., Democracy as a universal value, *Journal of Democracy,* 10 (3), 3–17, 1999.

_____. What's the point of democracy? *Bulletin of the American Academy of Arts and Sciences,* 57 (3), 8–11, 2004.

_____. *Development as Freedom,* Anchor Books, New York, 1999.

Sims, N., The art of literary journalism, in *Literary Journalism: A New Collection of the Best American Nonfiction,* Sims, N., Ed., Ballantine Books, New York, 1995.

Starr, P., *The Creation of the Media: Political Origins of Modern Communications,* Basic Books, New York, 2004.

Stepp, C.S., Journalism without profit margins, *American Journalism Review,* Oct./Nov., 37–43, 2004.

Strange, J.J. and Katz, E., The future of the fact, *Annals of the American Academy of Political and Social Science,* 560, 8–16, 1998.

Tocqueville, A., *Democracy in America* (1835); Vintage Books, New York, 1945.

Tuchman, G., Objectivity as strategic ritual: An examination of newsmen's notions of objectivity, *American Journal of Sociology,* 77, 660–679, 1972.

Vercic, D., The future: Technology, media and telecommunications (TMT) or dust, *Journalism Studies,* 2 (2), 291–294, 2001.

Ward, S., Pragmatic news objectivity: Objectivity with a human face, Discussion Paper D-37, The Joan Shorenstein Center on the Press, Politics and Public Policy, May 1999.

Westbrook, R.B., *John Dewey and American Democracy,* Cornell University Press, Ithaca, NY, 1991.

Woodward, G.C., Narrative form and the deceptions of modern journalism, in *Political Communication Ethics: An Oxymoron?* Denton Jr., R.E., Ed., Praeger, London, 2000.

Ziff, H.M., The closing of the journalistic mind, *Columbia Journalism Review,* Jan–Feb., 49–51, 1992.

Selected Bibliography: Journalism Education

Adam, G.S., A Provost's Advice on Bollinger's Quest, www.journalism.nyu. edu/pubzone/debate/forum.

_____. The education of journalists, *Journalism: Theory, Practice, and Criticism,* 2 (3), Dec., 315–339, 2001.

_____. James Carey's academy, in *James Carey: A Critical Reader,* Munson, E.S. and Warren, C.A., Eds., University of Minnesota Press, Minneapolis, 1997.

Association for Education in Mass Communication and Journalism, Challenges and Opportunities in Journalism and Mass Communication Education: A Report of the Task Force on Journalism and Mass Communication Education (AEJMC Task Force), *Journalism Educator,* 44 (12), A2–A24, 1989.

Becker, L.B., Training Reporters versus Educating Journalists, www.mtsu.edu/ ~masscom/seig96/bogart/becker.htm.

Bogart, L., The Changing Market for Journalism, www.mtsu.edu/~masscom/ seig96/bogart/bogart.htm.

Bollinger, L.C., Journalism Task Force Statement, April 2003, www.jrn.columbia.edu/news/2003-04/taskforce.asp.

Boroff, D., What Ails the Journalism Schools, *Harper's Magazine,* Oct., 77–85, 1965.

Boylan, J., *Pulitzer's School: Columbia University's School of Journalism, 1903–2003,* Columbia University Press, New York, 2003.

Bromley, M., Journalism Still Dodges the Big Questions: A View from Australia, www.journalism.nyu.edu/pubzone/debate/forum.

Campbell, C.C., One Heresy for Every Verity: What if Columbia's Team of Journalism All-Stars Went to School? www.journalism.nyu. edu/pubzone/debate/forum.

Campbell, R. Journalism Is Different, So Let's Get Rid of It, www.mtsu.edu/ ~masscom/seig96/medsger/campbell.htm.

Carey, J.W., Where Journalism Education Went Wrong, www.mtsu.edu/ ~masscomm/seig96/carey/carey.htm.

Cunningham, B., Searching for the perfect journalism school, *Columbia Journalism Review,* Nov.–Dec., 20–30, 2002.

Birkhead, D., Journalism education: Is there a more meaningful 'here' there? *Media Studies Journal,* Winter, 113–121, 1991.

De Burgh, H., Skills are not enough: The case for journalism as an academic discipline, *Journalism,* 4 (1), 95–112, 2003.

Dennis, E.E., Whatever happened to Marse Robert's dream? The dilemma of American journalism education, *Media Studies Journal,* 2, 1–22, 1988.

Dressel, P.L., *Liberal Education and Journalism,* Institute of Higher Education, Teachers College, Columbia University, New York, 1960.

Gaunt, P., The training of journalists in France, Britain and the U.S., *Journalism Quarterly,* 68, 582–588, 1988.

Glasser, T.L., What Difference Does a Journalism Education Make? www.journalism.nyu.edu/pubzone/debate/forum.

Goree, K., Teaching moral development in journalism education, *Journal of Mass Media Ethics,* 15 (2), 101–114, 2000.

Gregorian, V., Journalism, the Quintessential Knowledge Profession, has an Information Problem, www.journalism.nyu.edu/pubzone/debate/forum.

Gura, L., Journalism Is Thinkology: Now How Do You Teach That? www.journalism.nyu.edu/pubzone/debate/forum.

Henry, N., Journalism education: A lost cause? *Chronicle of Higher Education,* Sept. 25, 1998, pp. B8–B9.

Highton, J., Perhaps it's time to abolish journalism schools, *The Masthead* (National Conference of Editorial Writers), Winter, 31–34, 1988.

Hynes, T., U.S. journalism and journalism education at the beginning of the twenty-first century, *Journalism Studies,* 2 (2), 285–291, 2001.

Karan, K., Journalism education in India, *Journalism Studies,* 2 (2), 294–299, 2001.

Katz, J., Bollinger's Windbags Won't Do Much without the Young, www.journalism.nyu.edu/pubzone/debate/forum.

Kennedy, D., Strip It Down, Go Eclectic: J-School Should Stop Getting in the Way of a Real Education, www.journalism.nyu.edu/pubzone/debate/forum.

Kroeger, B., Journalism with a Scholar's Intent, www.journalism.nyu.edu/pubzone/debate/forum.1.essay.kroger.html.

Kunkel, T., What is journalism education? *American Journalism Review,* Jan.–Feb., 2003.

Kunkel, T. , Journalism requires wide exposure, *Quill,* July,17–18, 2002.

Kurpius, D.D. , Journalism Education: Missing the Democratic Connections. A Research Report for the Kettering Foundation. The Kettering Foundation, Dayton, OH, 2003.

Lambeth, E., Media Institutions and Their Public Obligations, www.mtsu.edu/~masscom/seig96/bogart/lambeth.htm.

Ledbetter, J., Bad news: The slow, sad sellout of journalism school, *Rolling Stone,* Oct. 16, 1997, pp. 73–81, 99–100.

Manoff, R., Democratic Journalism and the Republican Subject: Or, the Real American Dream and What Journalism Educators Can Do about It, www. journalism.nyu.edu/pubzone/debate/forum.

Medsger, B., Grove City and the Vatican rag: On journalism as a scholarly activity, *Gannett Center Journal,* Spring,61–67, 1988.

———. *Winds of Change: Challenges Confronting Journalism Education,* Freedom Forum, Arlington, VA, 1996.

Is Journalism Different? www.mtsu.edu/~masscom/seig96/medsger/medsger.htm.

Getting Journalism Education Out of the Way, www.journalism.nyu.edu/pubzone/debate/forum.1.essay.medsger.html.

Megwa, E.R., Democracy without citizens: the challenge for South African journalism education, *Journalism Studies,* 2 (2), 281–285, 2001.

Pulitzer, J., Jr., Planning a school of journalism – The basic concept, *North American Review,* 178, 641–680, 1904.

Reese, S.D., The progressive potential of journalism education: Recasting the academic vs. professional debate, *Harvard International Journal of Press/ Politics,* 4 (4), 70–94, 1999.

Robins, W., Wimps of the Roundtable and Other Challenges for Journalism Schools, www.journalism.nyu.edu/pubzone/debate/forum.

Rosen, J., Taking Bollinger's Course on the American Press, www.journalism. nyu.edu/pubzone/debate/forum.

Rosen, J., Making Society Intelligible and Inhabitable, www.mtsu.edu/ ~masscom/seig96/carey/rosen.htm.

Rosenbaum, R., Columbia's J-School Needs to Consider Trollopian Retooling, www.journalism.nyu.edu/pubzone/debate/forum.

Schell, O., Some Ruminations on Journalism Schools as Columbia Turns, www. journalism.nyu.edu/pubzone/debate/forum.1.essay.schell.html.

School of Journalism, University of Oregon, Planning for Curricular Change: A Report on the Future of Journalism and Mass Communication Education, University of Oregon School of Journalism, Eugene, 1984.

Schultz, T., Does education matter? Characteristics of journalists who went to graduate school, *Journalism,* 3 (2), 223–238, 2002.

Seelye, K.Q., Times are tough for news media, but journalism schools are still booming, *The New York Times,* May 15, 2006, pp. C1–8.

Serrin, W., Time to Retire All the Old Arguments about Journalism School, www.journalism.nyu.edu/pubzone/debate/forum.

Shafer, J. Can J-School Be Saved? Oct. 7, 2002, www.slate.msn.com.

Steiner, L., Journalism Curricula Are Themselves Stories, www.mtsu.edu/ ~masscom/seig96/carey/steiner.htm.

Stephens, M., A J-School Manifesto, www.journalism.nyu.edu/pubzone/debate/
	forum.1.essay.stephens.html.
Steyn, E. and De Beer, A.S., The level of journalism skills in South African
	media: A reason for concern within a developing democracy? *Journalism
	Studies,* 5 (3), 387–297, 2004.
Traub, J., The Crisis Is Not in Here, but Out There: Journalism as Pedagogy,
	www.journalism.nyu.edu/pubzone/debate/forum.
Wartella, E., The Devil Is Always in the Details, http://www.mtsu.edu/
	~masscomm/seig96/carey/wartella.htm.

Index